Dads Matter

Lynn,

Thanks for all your photos, positive energy and being a great dad.

Bob Hylton

Dads Matter

Principles, Lessons & Stories on the Remarkable Impact of Fathers

Bob Hazleton

Four Forty Four Press
Corvallis, Oregon

Four Forty Four Press
Corvallis, Oregon
www.BobHazleton.com

Published 2009
Printed in the United States of America

ISBN: 978-0-615-30382-6
Library of Congress Control Number: 2009930799

Editing by The Mighty Pen (www.MightyPenEditing.com)
Design by Jennifer Omner (www.ALLPublications.com)
Cover photo (Keith, Jesse, and Bob Hazleton) by Sherry Hazleton
   with touch up by Rachel Rudiger
Author photo by Karl Maasdam (www.karlmaasdam.com)

To my wife Sherry who insisted I be a Dad and to my sons Keith and Jesse who allowed me to experience the rewards of fatherhood.

Contents

–1–

Are Dads Really Needed?

ASIDE FROM NEEDING a sperm donor, you can have a child without a male. A child can certainly be raised without a father. There are a lot of single moms, aunts and uncles, and grandparents raising children without the dad in the picture. In Chapter Five, you will read three stories of people who grew up without dads in their lives.

My niece Kathy tells the story of not meeting her dad until she was eighteen and only after she sought him out. My long-time friend Rick shares his memories of watching his Dad die of a heart attack when Rick was just three. Finally, there's the story of Bill Ogle whose Dad just disappeared while flying a private plane on a business trip.

All three, Kathy, Rick, and Bill, appear to have successfully made it into adult life. Kathy has two daughters and a dedicated husband, runs her own business, and lives near her brother and sisters in Florida. Rick is a kind and giving person. He has been married for over thirty years, has two adult children, is a skilled electronic tech, and is an outstanding high school and college soccer referee. Bill spent some time in the military, is married, has one child, and is now an Associate Professor in the Biomedical Engineering Department at the University of Florida. Yet in each of their stories, they talk about wishing they knew their dads and about the impact, throughout their lives, of not having one. To these three, *not* having a dad really mattered.

There is no shortage of famous people who grew up without a dad in their lives. Bill Cosby was instrumental in telling his dad to leave the family because his dad just "visited the family to sleep, to not share anything, and to argue and cause trouble with Mom." ("Cosby, Poussaint On Merits Of Two Parents.") Yet Bill Cosby became a comedian, actor, author, and America's dad in the '80s in *The Cosby Show*.

How about President Barack Obama? His parents divorced when Barack was just two years old. Barack Sr. only saw his son one other time, when the younger Barack was ten years old. In his 1995 book, *Dreams From My Father* Barack Obama wrote, "He (Barack Sr.) had left Hawaii in 1963 when I was only two years old, so that as a child, I knew him only through the stories that my mother and grandparents told." (Page 3)

Yet growing up without a father, President Obama graduated with a BA from Columbia University; he then graduated with a Juris Doctor (JD) magna cum laude from Harvard in 1991. While at Harvard, he was editor and then president of the *Harvard Law Review*. He has been a professor at the University of Chicago Law School, a state legislator, and a U.S. senator of Illinois. So, sure, you don't necessarily need to have a father to become famous and successful.

Yet both Bill Cosby and President Obama call for the need of fathers and stress the importance for fathers to be in their kid's lives. Bill Cosby's 1986 book *Fatherhood* was a bestseller. His current book, *Come on, People*, co-written with Alvin F. Poussaint, stresses, among other things, the need for responsible fatherhood. Then-candidate Obama, in his 2008 Father's Day speech, called out to dads to have the courage to stick around and raise their children.

My own story as a dad took an unexpected turn when I sent my fifteen-year-old son Jesse to a program for troubled, defiant, and at-risk teens in Ensenada, Mexico. Because of this decision to intervene in my son's life, I became involved in the very program I sent Jesse to. I started working with other parents and saw many who had issues with their dads. Then I started working full time with the teens in the program. Time and time again, I encountered teens that were without their dads. Some of these teens had never seen or heard from their dads, other kids had lived with their dads, but he just wasn't available. These teens were of every national origin, every color, and every religious background imaginable— from boys from Egypt to girls from Korea to Iowa farm boys. They all wanted the same thing: to have their dads in their lives. To these teens, there was no question: their dads matter to them.

I was inspired to write this book because of all of the stories of pain and hurt I heard about people wanting their dads in their lives. I also wanted to explore why children and adults are so drawn to their dads in spite of many fathers being such cads. My hope is that this book will assist in shifting more dads into being responsible fathers.

What I hadn't planned on in the course of writing this book was discovering what it meant for me to be a dad and a son. I was surprised by how much I learned about both my relationship with my father and with my sons because of this book.

–2–

Dads Really Do Matter

A FOUR-YEAR-OLD GIRL wakes up in the middle of the night, crying for her dad. Mom comes into her room to comfort her, but the little girl keeps asking, "Why can't I see Daddy?" Mom is in her mid-twenties and has been a single mom since her daughter's birth. Dad moved over a hundred miles away and doesn't make much of an effort to see his daughter. Clearly, Dad matters to this child. But Dad doesn't seem to understand the impact his absence has on his daughter.

"I knew what I had to do. When my parents divorced, they didn't consider the impact on me and my brother. They actually put us in the middle of their divorce."

So what does this mom do? She understands that Dad matters, so she picks up and moved. That's right: she leaves her hometown of twenty-five years. She leaves her own parents behind and moves closer to her daughter's father, even though, as she says, he can be a jerk at times. Why is she willing to do this? Because Mom knows that this one dad mattered to her daughter.

A six-year-old gets all of his classmates to write letters to his Dad. Dad is a Navy ensign who was deployed to Iraq for seven months. When Dad comes back from Iraq, there is no airport reunion with signs, balloons, and hugs. Rather, Dad goes to his son's school as a surprise.

The YouTube video shows Dad coming into the back of the classroom. His son has his back to his father. When the boy senses something going on, he turns in his chair. Once he sees his dad, the boy bolts out of his chair and starts running toward him, arms spread wide. The boy is grinning then crying. Before the boy can get his arms around Dad's legs, Dad reaches down and swoops up his son. The boy buries his face into Dad's neck and just cries and cries and cries. ("Soldier surprises his six year old son in class.")

This dad understands what all kids want from their fathers: just love and affection. I recommend tissue paper before you watch this video: http://www.youtube.com/watch?v=UKWEphP2_Nw

During the weekend of Father's Day 2008, I witnessed three events that made it very clear that dads matter and that dads have an incredible impact on their adult children. The first was the death of Tim Russert of *NBC's Meet the Press*. The other two events were clips I saw on TV that involved Tiger Woods and Michael Jordan.

I paid a lot more attention to the news about Tim Russert when I heard that he and I were both born in May of 1950. That aside, I don't believe I have ever watched a single *Meet the Press* show, but I saw him moderate debates, and I have seen at least one of his books, *Letters from our Fathers*. In my limited knowledge of and exposure to Tim, I knew that his dad, "Big Russ," had a profound impact on him. In the interview replays after his death, I saw how important Tim's sons were to Tim. My impression was that Tim absolutely knew the impact that dads have on their kids, and he did everything he could to ensure he was there for his kids as a positive influence.

I got the impression Tim always saw the best in dads, too. In one interview, he had this goofy, semi-permanent smile on his face. He described a dad who worked long hours and was always gone to work before his kids got up to go to school. Tim looked like this gleeful little kid as he described how this dad left cute notes in his daughter's lunchbox.

I was saddened not only by the news of Tim Russert's death but by the timing. This wide eyed optimist, a dedicated father and son dying just after his birthday and the day before Father's Day. On Father's Day, I got up early to travel to Alexandria, Louisiana, to conduct two weeks of seminars at a specialty school for troubled teens.

When I got to the school, a school similar to the one Jesse attended for two years in Ensenada, Mexico, I immediately turned on the TV to watch golf's U.S. Open and to catch the fifth game of the NBA finals. During these telecasts, I saw two short clips about dads. The first clip was about Tiger Woods, narrated by Tiger's dad, Earl Woods. The senior Woods talked about how he kept challenging and pushing Tiger as a teen; heck, probably from the time he was born. What struck me was how Earl Woods was able to push Tiger to his limits without being an obsessive, over-the-top sports dads. Earl talked about dropping his golf clubs right in the middle of Tiger's backswing—he said Tiger would give him that glare he is now so famous for. But Earl said Tiger never let anything distract him in the course of a round of golf. Thankfully, Earl Woods wasn't trying to live his sports career through Tiger. I wish more sports dads would take Earl Woods's lead to influence and push their kids in sports, but not obsess over their sons' and daughters' careers.

Throughout his career, Tiger has praised the influence of his dad. If you follow golf, you know how much Tiger was affected by his dad's death. Earl D. Woods is listed first on the Board of Directors as "Chairman In Memoriam" on the Tiger Woods Foundation Web site. On the Web site, there is a nice picture of Earl Woods hanging on Tiger's arm.

The other short clip I saw was an interview with Michael Jordan. M. J. talked at length about how his dad, James Jordan, influenced him. M. J. also explained how his trip into minor league baseball was all about his dad, about a promise Michael made to his dad—a promise that many people didn't understand. What really amazed me was that M. J. said he was not bitter toward the men who killed his dad. M. J. also said that even after his dad's death, James Jordan has been an influence in his life.

There are not many dads who will have a famous newsman, or the world's best golfer, or the best basketball player of all time, as a son. But the good news is that any dad—*any* dad—can have as positive and powerful an influence on his kids as Big Russ, Earl Woods, or James Jordan did on theirs.

There are a lot of dads out there who fall way short of Big Russ, Earl Woods, and James Jordan. In my work with teens and their families, I see and hear about the negative impact that absent, oblivious, and abusive dads have on their kids. I have seen kids who are angry, bitter, and resentful that they have never seen or heard from their dads. I have seen the same reaction from kids whose dads are just barely in their lives.

A story by Jemele Hill appeared on ESPN.com entitled "Karl Malone's Shameful Secret," the story of a famous dad who just wasn't in his son's life. In fact, he refused to be in his son's life when given the chance.

> This is how Demetrius Bell—drafted a couple of weeks ago by the Buffalo Bills in the seventh round—describes his relationship with his father:
>
> "I treat it as if my mother went to the sperm bank. I don't hate him for [not being in my life]. It made me a better person."
>
> But it's pretty hard to reduce your father to a DNA dispenser when everyone else in the world knows him as

the NBA's second-leading scorer of all time, a two-time Olympic gold medalist, and arguably the greatest power forward ever.

Yes, Bell's father is Karl Malone. And if you are wondering why you never heard of Bell or seen these two engaged in any father-son moments, it's because Malone wants nothing to do with him . . .

It's hard to tell which is more astonishing: that Malone actually feels this way, or that Bell was able to overcome the heartbreaking reality of being rejected by a parent . . .

Bell lost out in the father lottery. (In my seminars, I tell kids in similar situations that they were dealt a lousy hand when it came to a father.) According to Bell, Malone told him it was too late for him to be his father, and he'd have to make it on his own.

Nice to meet you too, Dad . . .

What makes his apparent reluctance to be a father to Bell that much more astonishing is that Malone also grew up fatherless. Malone's father committed suicide when he was three. ("Karl Malone falls short, as a father.")

While Demetrius Bell seems to have come to grips with not having a dad in his life, that's not the reaction of teens I see in my seminars. I see boys angry and hurt that Dad abandoned them. I have heard story after story from girls saying they throw themselves at boys just to have a little male attention. What's really sad is many of these girls were treated poorly by abusive guys. Then there are the kids whose dads are there at home but are unavailable, both physically and emotionally—dads who are too busy with work, or, worse, who are abusing drugs and alcohol.

While it's great to see the positive influence of dads like Earl Woods, James Jordan, or Big Russ, I see far too many kids who have been negatively affected by their dads.

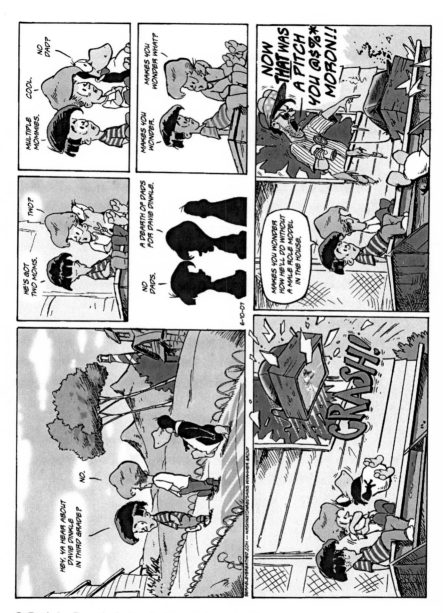

As I started writing this book, I came across an Opus comic that had quiet the message about dads. If it weren't so true, it wouldn't be so funny *and* so sad. I think the dad, the male influence depicted here, is only a slight exaggeration of real-life, beer-drinking, violent, sports-obsessed dads. The comic implies that kids would be better off without a dad. Maybe they would be better off without a dad like that. But kids want—and, in my opinion, need—their dads.

The dad depicted in the comic has just as much of an impact on his child as Big Russ, Earl Woods, and James Jordan had on theirs. Why? Because, as I have seen over and over, kids have a natural and extremely strong attraction to their dads, whether Dad is awesome or awful.

Yet how are dads portrayed today? As I was growing up, I saw the image of Dad, of families in general, as perfect without fault in shows like *Father Knows Best* and *Leave it to Beaver.* As I grew older, the portrayal of dads went to *Dr. Huxtable* in *The Cosby Show,* then degraded to Al Bundy in *Married with Children,* and then slipped still again to Homer Simpson.

I'm not sure I like this trend.

I saw a card a few days before Father's Day 2008 in a little gift shop at a resort in Midway, Utah. Two things struck me: the 1950s dad and the big message:

IT'S GOOD TO
BE A DAD!

As I leaned in to take a closer look at the card, I saw the fine print between the big bold print:

IT'S GOOD TO
have money out the wazoo if you plan to
BE A DAD!

The clincher was the inside message:

Happy Father's Day
to my favorite ATM

The message is: Dad is just there to provide money.

Today it seems like dads are portrayed as bumbling nerds who just get by in life. I even saw this sentiment in my local paper:

> We hereby deliver **ROSES** to Dad. Sunday is his day, and although he might prefer a somewhat less flowery tribute, we leave it to family members to honor him in the way that would be most meaningful. And by "him" we also include stepdads and uncles and brothers who also step into the role of mentor to children whose fathers are absent for whatever reason.
>
> Dads who step up don't get their fair share of tribute these days, and they may tire of being so routinely seeing themselves depicted as bungling, insensitive, and largely irrelevant members of the family (or worse). In real life, we know that devoted fathers who go out of their way to nurture and advise and support their children should be appreciated every day. (Roses and Rasberries)

I couldn't agree more that dads are portrayed as bumbling doofuses on TV. It's the general trend of emasculating of dads on TV and in advertising. There is a guy I have seen in a number of TV commercials that typifies how dads are currently being portrayed.

In a Verizon commercial, he comes out of his house (with the Verizon crew in tow, of course), confidently talking about all the projects he is going to take on. As he gets away from his house, he starts strutting and getting louder and more confident. Just as he's getting into stride, his young teen daughter says, "Dad!" In her tone I hear, "Don't be so embarrassing," "Why can't you be normal?" and "Please don't act like that around me."

In the Home Depot commercial, he's about to take on the simple project of hanging something on the wall in the living room. His wife seems wary of him doing any home improvement project. He triumphs in completing this simple project, and his wife pats him on the back, as if he has made a major accomplishment. In a Washington Mutual ad, he comes off with some false bravado when he opens an account anyone can have.

I have to admit, we dads bring a lot of this incompetent image on ourselves. Some of the tasks in my house tend to fall along traditional gender lines. For instance, if my family has any kind of rodent problem (mice or rats), it's definitely my job to take care of it. Once I came home from work on a hot August afternoon and Sherry greeted me with, "The dogs left you a present in the backyard." It was a dead possum! But I know that when I do the simplest of home repairs—replacing the toilet float, for example—I go on and on about how skilled I am. If my wife Sherry went on like that every time she made dinner or did the laundry, I would go nuts and tell her to cut it out.

I realize these portrayals of dads hardly measure up to the degrading portrayals and images of women or minorities we've seen over the years, but it sets up a dichotomy. On TV, dads are shown as helpless, goofy, and barely able to dress themselves. Yet in my seminars, I see kids devastated when their dads are not in their lives.

I don't fully understand it, but I see it all the time. Dads have an incredible power with their kids. To me, this power is most evident in kids who have had no dad, or who just have a dad who is awful. Kids want to know and see their dads, even when their dad has never been in their lives. Kids whose dads have done the most awful things will still defend their dads. I have heard kids defend their dads who are in prison or who are drug dealers.

In his book *A Wolf at the Table,* Augusten Burroughs describes a similar theme. Augusten spends most of his life seeking Dad's approval and attention, in spite of the fact that his dad not only didn't show any affection, but also tormented his boy. Augusten was still haunted by his dad even after his dad died. (Burroughs)

The most confounding phenomena to me are kids who were abandoned by their dads at a very early age and yet still want to search out and find them. I have personal experience with this one with my niece Kathy, but it doesn't make it any easier for me to comprehend.

In this book, I will relate Kathy's and many other true stories to show the powerful draw and impact dads have on their kids' early and adult lives.

–3–

The Seminars
and the Program

All of your behavior results from the thoughts that precede it.
DR. WAYNE W. DYER

I'LL REFER TO "the program" and "the seminars" through-out this book. For my youngest son Jesse, "the program" was a specialty school in Ensenada, Mexico that he attended for twenty-six months. There, he learned about himself and why he was going down a self-destructive path. After dropping out of tenth grade in public school, he completed the tenth, eleventh, and twelfth grades in fewer than two years. He graduated with a GPA in excess of 3.5 and was recognized as an honor graduate.

For Sherry and me, as well as thousands of other parents, the program was the choice of last resort. Program teens tend to be involved in drugs, skipping or doing poorly in school, getting into trouble with the police, and stealing from their parents.

The program schools are a loose affiliation of specialty schools for at-risk, defiant, and troubled teens. These schools are an alternative for parents who have run out of options for their teenagers. They see their teens' lives sliding into drug addiction, juvie or jail, homelessness, or, worse, death!

Parents are desperate to save their children's lives. The program does just that—it saves teens' lives, and it brings families back together.

Sherry and I tried so many options. I followed Jesse around at school for two days in the eighth grade after a drug-related suspension. I took Jesse, kicking and screaming, for a drug test. We called the police several times when he ran away. Once, five police cars screeched up to our house when Sherry called 9-1-1 and Jesse screamed on the phone and slammed the receiver down. We tried to get Jesse to see a counselor, but he refused. We had an intervention at his high school, but he didn't show up. We didn't know what to do. We actually hired a transport company to take Jesse to a lockdown drug rehab facility in Gresham, Oregon, and then we sent him to a newly opened program school in Ensenada, Mexico.

Yes, the schools can be tough. The teens wear uniforms. They must stand in straight lines when going from place to place. They count off when they go through doors to ensure no one has run off. Boys and girls are separated at all times. Boys aren't allowed to look at girls, and vice versa. None of the teens are allowed to even look out of a window. They are required to go to school and actually study. They do jobs—chores, of all things! They go to bed and wake up at set times. Yes, there is serious structure.

The program is a results-based program. Kids are not in the program for a set amount of time. The teens have to show results to advance through the program. At the lower levels, there are very few privileges or responsibilities. As teens progress up the levels, both their privileges and their responsibilities increase. The teens dictate just how long the program takes.

The unique feature of this particular program is that it addresses the entire family dynamic. The basic concept is, if a teen makes changes while in the program and is sent back home to the identical family dynamic, there is no support for the teen's change. Without this family support, the teen's old behavior will eventually return. If the teen's environment hasn't changed, it makes it harder for the teen's change to be permanent.

One of the vehicles for working with the parents and addressing the family dynamic is the seminars. The seminars are conducted by Premier Educational Seminars, Inc. and are specifically designed for at-risk teens and their families. The seminars have been labeled personal- or self-growth seminars, or awareness training or self-improvement seminars. My son Keith, who also attended the Premier Seminars, called them emotional boot camp. In the seminars, you explore what makes you do the things you do. What is it that makes you tick? Why are you the way you are? You get a good close look at what has been working and what hasn't been working in your life, then you find ways to be the person you really want to be.

Sherry and I attended all the Premier Seminars offered at the time. Sherry was so apprehensive that, before the first seminar, she hoped she would catch pneumonia so she wouldn't have to attend. But we did go to the seminars, and we got a lot out of them. Just like many of the parents, we initially went to the seminars hoping to make Jesse "better." But we found that we had been carrying around a lot of psychological baggage ourselves.

We took a close look at the roles we played in our family. I acted as the judge, jury, and executioner when it came to discipline. Sherry was always intervening and acted as the negotiator and peace-maker. As a result of these seminars, our marriage improved. Sherry gained more self-confidence.

Some people, like me, make significant changes in their lives as a result of taking on the seminar material. After attending all of my seminars, I started to staff the seminars, assisting the seminar facilitator and the attendees. I then participated in ten-month life-coach training. I followed that training as staff for another life-coaching training. I then spent a year in training as a seminar facilitator. Finally, I quit my job as an engineer and became a facilitator of the teen seminars.

Other people, such as Sherry, make more subtle changes. After quitting her job and taking six months off, Sherry initially planned to do some volunteer work at the hospital where she'd worked. But after taking a seminar called Visions, she decided she wanted to be paid. Sherry wrote a proposal to work in a department that had previously only hired registered nurses, which she wasn't. Sherry not only got the job, but she insisted on only working part-time. Rather than taking a job determined by others, Sherry created the exact job she wanted.

But the material presented in the seminars is not necessarily unique. There are lots of companies out there conducting similar seminars and programs. I went to a seminar by Landmark Education called the Forum. The architecture firm I work for provides their employees the opportunity to attend seminars by PSI International. There are many other companies offering similar seminars.

Much of the material presented in the Premier Seminars can be found in the self-help material available to the general public. Dr. Phil, Steven Covey, Dr. Wayne Dyer, and Rhonda Byrne (author of *The Secret*) use similar concepts to those presented in the Premier Seminars.

Bill Cosby and Alvin F. Poussaint wrote *Come on, People: On the Path from Victims to Victors*. In addition to discussions of parenting, the book includes a message: don't be a victim (Cosby and Poussaint).

We have a fun exercise in the Premier Seminars about being victims. The seminar participants are paired up and each person gets a chance to share a story where they felt they were the victim: an event where they felt all the forces of the universe conspired against them. I tell the participant to lay it on thick, to embellish whenever possible. Don't let the facts get in the way of a good victim story. At the end of their victim story, their partner puts up two fingers to make a "V" symbol, places their hand on their forehead and sighs, "Ahhh, poor victim." The real work comes when I ask the participants to retell their stories in an accountable manner. I ask them to talk about their assumptions, what they were unconscious of, what they were in denial of, and what they avoided saying or doing. Generally, the accountable version of the story is shorter than the victim story because it is just the facts. People also tend to find the accountable story a little harder to tell. Why? Because they have a lot more practice being a victim than being accountable.

I recently read Cesar Millan's *Be the Pack Leader*. Cesar introduces the concepts of your way of being, the energy you project, having clean and positive intention, self-talk/inner dialogue, and positive affirmations—all concepts that are covered in the Premier Seminars. Cesar also refers to Deepak Chopra and Wayne Dyer.

Cesar also wrote an article entitled "What Your Pet Can Teach You," for the January 11, 2009 issue of *Parade* magazine. Among the eight points he made, he included:

Live in the moment

Be direct and consistent with your communication

Learn to listen

Live with purpose (10)

Again, these are all concepts we cover in the seminars. How about Don Miguel Ruiz's *The Four Agreements*? They are:

Be impeccable with your word

Don't take anything personally

Don't make assumptions

Always do your best

Again, we cover these concepts in the seminars. The concepts presented in the Premier Seminars are pretty mainstream and used by many other people. We just package the presentations for troubled teens and their families. The two biggest and most basic concepts we cover are about beliefs and attitude. The concept "behavior follows beliefs" is the centerpiece of the seminars. This simply means that all of your behaviors reinforce a belief you have, especially about yourself. If you believe you are shy, you avoid contact with people. If you believe you are outgoing, you go out of your way to interact with people.

Henry Ford put it like this: "If you think you can do a thing or think you can't do a thing, you're right."

The other major concept is about personal choice. It's about choosing our attitude, moment to moment. Every attitude we have—sadness, joy, resignation, confidence—is a choice we make. These choices may be made unconsciously, but they are our choices nonetheless. The example I use in the seminars is that of Holocaust survivor and author of *Man's Search for Meaning*, Viktor Frankl.

His quote concerning attitude is astounding, considering his time in a concentration camp: ". . . everything can be taken from a man but one thing: the last of the human freedoms—to choose one's attitude in any given set of circumstances, to choose one's own way." (66)

Consider a less extreme example: you come home from a long day at work and a longer commute home from work. You're tired, worn out, and grouchy. All you want to do is relax, lie on the couch, and close your eyes. Now one of your kids asks you to take them and five friends to loud and noisy Chuck E. Cheese. Not what you had in mind. What's your attitude? What's your energy level? But what if when you get home, you have a surprise chance to do something you really like? Now what's your attitude, your energy level? Both of your attitudes are choices—choices that you have made.

This is exactly what is presented in the seminars: making internal changes—changes in the beliefs you have about yourself—and making choices about your attitude. But the unique feature of the seminars put together by Premier Educational Seminars is that the seminars are specifically designed for these at-risk teens and their families.

I have seen and experienced amazing transformation as a result of these seminars in both teens and parents. Some people have made huge changes in their lives. Some people continue to do the same things, but they say that their entire attitudes toward family, friends, work, coworkers—toward life—has shifted.

I am one of those people who experienced a transformation in my life and what I do. I received a degree in mechanical engineering from the University of Maryland in 1972. From the moment I graduated until March 2006 I made a living as an engineer. In April 2006, I quit my job and became a seminar facilitator.

There weren't a lot of logical reasons for me to make this leap into a new career. Initially, my pay was cut by more than half. I no longer had an employer-paid health plan or a 401(k). I was away from home for two weeks at a time. I worked six long days in a row, had one day off, and then worked five more days. I traveled across the country; my accommodations were modest, and I dealt with teens that were big pains in the rear.

To say I was making a difference or giving back is too simple and trite. I don't know if it's my cynical nature (or is it my skepticism?), but I don't like to make a big deal about what I do.

But there are some things about my behavior that are undeniable. I do notice how excited I get as I approach a training. My wife also noticed how grumpy I get when I was home too long. While at the end of a two-week training I feel I'm dragging myself out of bed. But when the training starts, I always have energy and get excited. Once I shivered through two days of training with a fever, nausea, and diarrhea. In my engineering work, I could have legitimately called in sick those two days. But it never occurred to me to call off a training when so much depended on me.

In every seminar I have attended and facilitated, I have encountered people who have issues around Dad. In one seminar, I was working with a mom after she unsuccessfully attempted to solve a simple puzzle. I asked her what was going on, how she was feeling.

She said, "I feel stupid." I then simply asked her, "who was the first person that called you stupid?"

The expression on her faced didn't change, yet everything about her changed. Her body stiffened, she had a look that said something was brewing, but she didn't want it to show. Her eyes got wet and shiny. Her chin started to quiver. I could tell she was mightily trying to hold something back. She bit her lip, a single tear dropped down her check. Finally, she just said, "my dad," and burst into tears. This intelligent, capable woman had spent several decades believing she was stupid because something her dad told her.

The experience of seeing so many people with dad issues was my motivation for writing this book. I hope that dads will see how important they are, that they will realize they matter and be the dad they know they can be.

–4–

What Kind of Dad Do You Want to *Be*?

I STARTED THIS book project thinking that I would be writing a how-to-be-a-dad book. But the way most how-to books are written is that a problem is described and then a solution or step-by-step instructions are given. If you want to build a deck or repair plumbing that is the kind of book you want. There seems to be a "For Dummies" book written for every possible subject.

I have seen a number of books out there on parenting and being a dad that use this approach. I even refer to several of these books and resources at the end of this book. I saw a book that used this approach by Dr. Lee Parrott III entitled, *Helping Your Struggling Teen, A Parenting Guide on Thirty-Six Common Problems.*

The problem I see with this approach is that there is no way to detail all the possible scenarios that could come up being a dad. Besides, what we are dealing with here is human behavior, which is complicated, unpredictable, tricky business. There is no one solution to a problem that will work with every child. My sons were quite different from each other. What worked with Keith didn't necessarily work with Jesse.

Dr. Parrott's book and others are fine resources; this book, however, does not take the how-to approach. I will offer some advice and suggestions, but by and large, this is a how *to Be* a dad book—and the emphasis is on *Be*.

So how do you want to *Be* as a dad? That question sounds a little weird. How about this? What kind of dad do you want to *Be*?

Be is deliberately capitalized. We are always *Being* something. It's just that most of us don't put much time or conscious effort into how we *Be*. Most of us just go through life *Doing* our thing, saying, "this is just the way I am" as if there is nothing we can do about how we *Be*.

So just what is *Being*? *Being* is our basic or essential nature. *Being* is who we are. It is *not* what we do, or what we have. It is the energy we project, and we are always projecting some sort of energy. Have you ever had the experience of seeing someone for the first time and being able to tell if they are happy or sad, powerful or timid, outgoing or shy?

I found a straightforward, practical article discussion of the energy we project in the unlikeliest of places—in Cesar Millan's *Be the Pack Leader*. In his *Dog Whisperer* show, Cesar says that dogs pick up on our energy. In both his show and in his book, Cesar spends half of his attention on how the human is being with the dog before he will actually work with the dog. He goes on to say that when and only when humans project calm, assertive energy can we become the pack leader. You could almost substitute "children" for "dog" or "pet" and everything Cesar says would still apply (except the discussion on selecting types of collars!).

As a real-life example of how certain people *Be*, and of the energy they project, I love the sports analogies, so let me compare two current golfers: Tiger Woods and Phil Mickelson. How does Tiger show up in golf tournaments? He is singularly focused; he is determined. He doesn't talk a lot with his playing partner; he doesn't smile when he is in a tough competition. Look at his focus and determination in the 2008 U.S. Open. He was injured with a knee that hurt and a stress fracture that ended his 2008 season. But he didn't complain or whine. He essentially put his head down and went about his business. Tiger is focused on being the greatest golfer in the world, the greatest golfer of *all* time.

Tiger would probably take on *any* task or career in this focused and determined way. This is who he is. This is Tiger's way of *Being*.

Now consider Phil Mickelson. He's another great golfer, but his way of *Being* is much different than Tiger's. Phil takes a lot of chances on the golf course. He plays to the crowd. He is very popular; fans really like Phil Mickelson. When he won his first Master title, people were thrilled for him. His family was right there for his victory celebration. Fans *like* Phil, but they *admire* Tiger and his ability. They each have a different way of *Being*. Neither is better or worse than the other; they are just different.

How about the difference between Will Ferrell and Colin Farrell? They are both actors, but it is clear that they each have a different way of *Being*. I don't know if Colin could ever pull off some of the comedy roles Will has had.

While I was visiting Mark Twain's boyhood home in Hannibal, Missouri I saw the following quote that was attributed to him:

> *A person's nature never changes. What it is in childhood,*
> *it remains under pressure . . . it can partially or wholly*

disappear from sight, and for considerable stretches of time, but nothing can ever modify it, nothing can remove it.

I believe Mark Twain is referring to our inherent instinctual way of *Being* as a child. What I see Mark Twain saying is that, as children, we were born with a certain way of *Being*. Then as we grow older, this natural way of *Being* disappears or gets covered up. As we grow older, we unconsciously create other ways of *Being* to cope and survive, first as teens and then as adults.

We all show up in relationships in a certain way. This way of *Being* is automatic, it's instinctive, it's habit. We react, respond, and behave in certain ways without even thinking about it. A lot of how we *Be* is done at an unconscious level.

In his compelling book *Blink,* Malcolm Gladwell addresses the issue of humans' unconsciousness. He called it "adaptive conscious." Mr. Gladwell examines not just how powerful our adaptive conscious is, but also just how much and how often it controls our decisions and behaviors. Mr. Gladwell references an Implicit Association Test (IAT), an example of which can be found at www.implicit.harvard.edu. This test measures our "second level attitude . . . on an unconscious level—the immediate, automatic associations that tumble out before we've even had time to think." (84–85)

The disturbing thing about the test is that it shows that our unconscious attitudes may be utterly incompatible with our stated values.

So how many dads have sat down and considered this question: What kind of dad do I want to *Be*?

I know I didn't.

In fact, as I became a dad, all I remember thinking was

that there were certain things I didn't ever want to *do* to my kids—but I was reacting to things that happened to me as a kid. A lot of us dads say we didn't like this or that about our dads. We often don't see or even admit what good examples and lessons our dads provided for us.

Here's an example I heard in one of my seminars: John shared that his dad was just not a good father. John's dad drank, he didn't hold down a job, and, apparently, he didn't provide any emotional support for John. So when John became a dad, he decided he didn't want to be anything like his dad. In fact, he decided to be just the opposite. So what did John do? He worked *all* the time—but he didn't drink. His work became his addiction. John figured that if he bought things for his son, that would show how much he cared for him. Guess what? It didn't work at all for his son. John's son just wanted time with his dad.

There's an expression I use many times in my trainings: 180 degrees of not working is still not working. John illustrated this point so well. He decided to be 180 degrees different (the exact opposite) from his dad. But it didn't work for his son. Instead of looking at what he wanted to create, he decided what he didn't want. John did succeed; he was nothing like his own father. And he wasn't the dad he really wanted to *Be*.

Often dads come to think that what they *do* defines who they are, or who they *Be*. Consider the example of the athlete who is obsessed with his career. His entire self-esteem is based on *Being* an athlete. Then, when a debilitating injury ended his career early, his entire life and self-esteem come crashing down around him. His self-esteem was based upon what he did, rather than who he is, who he *Be!*

I had an experience like this. I worked as an engineer for over thirty years, competent in the niche I created. Then I quit that familiar work and became a seminar facilitator. The first time I got up in front a bunch of teens I was, frankly, awful. It's funny to think back on that now, but at the time, I really beat up on myself. I had based my worth on what I did. As an engineer, I could stand tall and proud. It took a lot of work to get my engineering degree and to work in the field for thirty years. When people asked me what I did, I said "I am a mechanical engineer," and that was it. I had instant credibility; it was all I needed to say. But when I felt I was incompetent as a facilitator, it was more than a little unsettling. The same thing happens to guys when they feel they have made a mistake as a dad. But it's not the mistakes or our past that defines us, it's how we respond to life's challenges.

So how do you find out who you want to *Be*? First, take stock of yourself now—who you *Be*. Get a journal and write the qualities you see in yourself now; then write the qualities you desire. How do you find out if you are really living the qualities you desire? Start noticing your language, your behaviors, your mood, and how people respond to you. Then ask for feedback from someone who is willing to be very honest with you. Sherry does a nice job of giving me direct, honest feedback.

So often we can't see or are unwilling to see ourselves as others see us; it's called denial. Denial is a common and very powerful human trait. The other thing that works against people is that we often think of ourselves as what we want to *Be* and not who we are truly *Being*. In working with teens and families, I have found that people will often see themselves as they wish and hope they are, rather than how they really are. This is the concept I was referring to earlier when I mentioned Gladwell's book *Blink*—our conscious, practical mind may rationalize behaviors driven by our unconscious mind or adaptive conscious.

Once you have a good idea of how you are currently *Being*, decide if this is how you want to *Be*. Notice the qualities you want in yourself, or the qualities you admire in others. Then put these qualities to paper. Make a list. Next to each quality that you like write, write what it would look like for you to live that quality.

Once you have a good, solid list that gives you an understanding of what living these qualities will look like, focus on each quality, one at a time. I pick one or two of these qualities a day to focus on. As I go through the day, I remind myself of the qualities I am focusing on. At the end of the day, I journal on what I noticed about myself and these qualities in me. Another simple exercise is to simply pause several times during the day and just notice your mood; what's your energy? These simple processes can become a regular daily practice, something you can incorporate, just like getting up and brushing your teeth or having your morning cup of coffee.

Why?

Because you want to be more conscious of how you are showing up as a dad. When we show up as a jerk, or as impatient or cruel or insensitive, it's not because we consciously decided, "That is how I am going to be today." It tends to be an unconscious, automatic behavior. By consciously deciding what kind of dad you want to *Be*, you can *Be* that way no matter what your mood is. Going through this process can assist you in *Being* more aware of the energy you are projecting (who you are *Being*) from moment to moment.

Being Dad is not about the things you do or the things you provide to your kids. Too many dads I meet think if they give their kids stuff or do the right things with their kids, they will be good dads. If you are truly *Being* yourself, you will do the important things as a dad. Finally, dads, you don't have to give up your masculinity or machismo to be the dad you want to be.

You can still be a man *and* be sensitive or vulnerable. I assure you, you don't have to do yoga, listen to Enya, or watch Oprah to be the dad you really want to *Be*.

–5–

Actually Be There

THIS STATEMENT IS going to sound obvious, but too many men don't do this one simple thing: if you have a child, actually hang around and really be in their lives. Before you can be a dad you have to physically be there.

This is not complicated stuff!

With all privileges come responsibilities. In most cases, the responsibility far outweighs the privilege. Think about the privilege of driving a car. With this simple privilege comes some awesome responsibilities: driving safely, having insurance, and keeping the car maintained, to mention just a few.

There is a huge responsibility in being part of bringing a human life into the world. Think about it: with the privilege of making love, or having sex, comes the huge responsibility of actually being around for a minimum of twenty or so years and raising your own child. Barack Obama said it well in his 2008 Father's Day speech: "We need fathers to recognize their responsibility doesn't end at conception. That doesn't make you a father. What makes you a father isn't your ability to have a child. Any fool can have a child. That doesn't make you a father. It's the courage to raise a child that makes you a father."

Barack Obama grew up without a dad, yet he recognizes the importance of dads. Perhaps he can see this importance clearer than those who did grow up with a dad.

In each of my seminars, without fail, there are a number of teens who either don't know who or where their biological dads are, never actually had their biological dads in their lives at all, or just barely had their biological dads in their lives. Here's one example that's just a killer. After having a child, Dad gets divorced and remarried. Then he has children with his second wife. Dad is there for his second set of kids, but ignores the children from his first marriage. When I have heard teens share their stories about this situation, they have actually referred to this other family as "my dad's family." This language implies that their dad has moved on and has essentially divorced not only his wife, but his kids as well. Yikes!

In his book *Beautiful Boy*, a memoir about his son's drug addiction, David Sheff cites a study that found that 85 percent of children of divorce were heavy users of drugs in high school compared to 24 percent of those from intact families. (177)

Here's how a child's mind works: once you're my dad, you're always my dad. Divorcing your child does not work!

To me, it is just amazing how many teens respond with "I don't know" when I ask, "Where is your dad?" The stories are varied: Dad abandoned me and Mom when I was an infant; Dad divorced Mom and started his own family, or just disappeared; Dad is in prison (I hear this story a lot more often than you would think). Or the teens simply do not know the full story of their dads. All they know is that their biological dads have never been in their lives. Of course, there's the, "I was adopted" story. But in all cases, there's a common theme: the kids want to know the answer to a few basic questions:

Why?

What did I do wrong?

Did he love me?

What's the matter with me?

I have heard it over and over again: kids say they want to just find their dads and ask these questions. I am amazed when I hear the teens say they just want to see if their "real" dad loved them. I am totally baffled with this question. I've said a number of times, "Your dad has given you a message for eighteen years by making no effort to be around. Why is it that you need to actually hear it from him?" Yet I encounter this need, this desire, and this hunger in teens to find and talk to their dads. I have come to realize that kids must have a basic instinctual need to have their dads in their lives.

But how do kids react when their dads are not in their lives? It may be an oversimplification, but I generally see girls trying to find acceptance and love from males. And I generally see boys getting angry and lashing out at anyone near them to cover up the hurt.

Now I admit that these kids have an idealized view of what life would be like with their dads. The teens say things like, "I just wanted to play catch with Dad," or, "I just wanted Dad to take me to do father and son things." I heard one girl say that when she saw a dad at a park toss his daughter up in the air and catch her, she missed having that in her life. But all these teens can do is fantasize about their dads. Teens without dads make up what it would be like to have their "real" dads. Amazingly, these teens see the possibility of a relationship with their estranged dad in the most optimistic light.

The way girls go out looking for love and acceptance from boys is just amazing to me. Girls will literally throw themselves at boys—any boys—who show them any kind of attention. Some girls go for the older guys, adult men in their twenties or even thirties. What really gets me is how girls answer the question I always ask: "So just how does your so-called boyfriend treat you?" The answer is almost always some form of "very badly." These girls put up with all kinds of verbal and physical abuse. They do anything the boys (or men) ask them to do sexually; they take beatings; they will let their boyfriends dictate every aspect of their lives, including who they are allowed to talk to. All because, according to these girls, they want love, attention, and acceptance from a male because Dad was not there to give them attention. Girls have actually said to me: "Well, if my dad abused and abandoned me, why not let boys do the same thing?"

As for boys—wow! Have I ever run across some angry young men in my seminars! These boys got hurt by Dad at an early age. So what do they do? They put up a front, a façade that says, "Hey, I am tough, and I will not let anyone get close." When they get angry, they tend to lash out at those closest to them, especially their moms. This really gets me. Mom has been around the entire time, but because Dad wasn't there, Mom gets the brunt of the boy's anger.

I have also heard boys say that if they ever see their dad, they will kill him. I've heard a boy actually say that he would be willing to do life in prison to have the pain go away. But even if he could kill Dad, I don't think the pain would go away.

A lot of these boys don't let stepdads get close at all. The boys say it's a case of loyalty. "If I let my stepdad into my life, I am being disloyal to my dad." Disloyal to a dad who has never been there! Amazing!

When a boy is able to get past his anger and let down his tough-guy image, he will actually show some emotion about not having his dad around. I have held a number of teen boys in my arms who just sob, asking over and over, "Why? I just want to know why!"

Amazingly, these teens, both boys and girls, go and search out their dads when they get older. The draw or the power of Dad is so strong; I have heard kids defend dads who are frankly pretty awful. I have heard teens make excuses for their dads who are in prison.

I have known teens who do not want to speak poorly of their drug-dealing dads. This may be about the teens being embarrassed that they have a dad who is in prison. Yet many of the teens I deal with seem to be following the path their dads have taken: doing drugs, being violent, and getting into trouble with the law. If this doesn't show how powerful and influential dads are, I don't know what does.

But what about longer-term effects? I read two pieces that really struck me. One was in Tony Dungy's book, *Quiet Strength*. Coach Dungy talks about his ability to rally interest and enthusiasm around things that were important to him:

> One of those things was the All Pro Dad organization, which I founded with Mark Merrill and Clyde Christensen. Our original goal was to try and reach dads everywhere, whether in the city or the suburbs, married or single. Our message was simple: dads—including us—need to spend more time with their kids. In four short years, All Pro Dad had grown into a national organization that sponsored clinics—called All Pro Dad Father & Kid Experiences—in NFL cities across the country and sent daily tips via email to fathers around the nation.
>
> As Mark studied life in the United States, he had

*learned that two-thirds of African American teens have
absent fathers. And I had learned from visiting prisons
that the most common factor among male inmates was
growing up without a dad in the home. When we put
those two facts together, we knew we needed to focus
our attention on fathers. (199)*

Coach Dungy is being kind when he uses the term "absent dad." I suppose the term "absent" is technically correct, but it is too neutral. Given the sadness, anger, and feelings of abandonment I see the teens in my seminars experiencing, I would use stronger language.

Roland Martin of CNN.com did just that when he addressed a similar topic in his December 11, 2007 CNN.com column, "Commentary: Black men must reclaim our children" about the murder of Washington Redskins cornerback, Sean Taylor:

*As the mug shots of the alleged killers of NFL star Sean
Taylor were shown on television, I kept wondering when
we were going to see their parents step forward. I saw
a couple of mothers, but their dads were missing in
action.*

*Dads matter, and it's ridiculous for us to act as if all it
takes is a loving mom . . .*

*We can spend all day talking about the ills afflicting
urban America—and there are plenty that are institutional—but the decaying value of life in inner cities
clearly can be traced to the exodus of fathers from the
lives of so many young men. Excuses often are tossed*

about as to why black men leave their children (and their children's moms) to fend for themselves. But a lot of them are just sorry and refuse to accept the responsibility that comes with raising a child.

A lot of my colleagues will suggest it's too simplistic to assign such a high value to a dad being in the life of a child. But just take a visit to your local jail, juvenile hall, or state prison. You likely will be confronted with a sea of black men—strong, able-bodied, creative, and restless—who have spent or will spend years and years with a prison number identifying who they are . . .

But you see, when nearly 70 percent of black kids are born to unmarried parents, likely to a too-young mom, that puts tremendous pressure on grandmothers (and some grandfathers), sisters, and brothers to take up the slack. But if the person who impregnated that woman were on the scene, not only helping to pay for the raising of the child, but also serving as a strong influence, I just don't believe we would see such a chronic condition . . .

A friend of mine suggested more black men need to mentor young black men. I agree. But that's a bandage. If we get black men to handle their business in the first place, no one else would have to stand in the gap.

Unless black America owns up to this problem—and fast—we are going to see another generation of young black men who are angry with their lot in life. And the result will be more discipline problems in school, which will lead to folks dropping out, and that is nothing but a one-way ticket to jail.

Black men, it's time to man up. Enough with the sperm donors. We need real men to stand up and accept

> *their responsibility. The state of our boys is on us and no one else.*

Here's more of Barack Obama's Father's Day speech, which carries a similar message:

> *But if we are honest with ourselves, we'll admit that too many fathers also are missing—missing from too many lives and too many homes. They have abandoned their responsibilities, acting like boys instead of men. And the foundations of our families are weaker because of it.*
>
> *You and I know how true this is in the African-American community. We know that more than half of all black children live in single-parent households, a number that has doubled—doubled—since we were children. We know the statistics—that children who grow up without a father are five times more likely to live in poverty and commit crime; nine times more likely to drop out of schools and twenty times more likely to end up in prison. They are more likely to have behavioral problems, or run away from home, or become teenage parents themselves. And the foundations of our community are weaker because of it.*

Coach Dungy, Mr. Martin, and Barack Obama, who are all African-American, seem to see this absent-dad thing as a black phenomenon. Given what I see in my seminars, the absent dad issue is color-blind. I see white, black, Hispanic, and Asian kids all suffer the pain of having an absent dad. Lately in my seminars, I have seen more and more Eastern European teens without their biological dads in their lives.

Roland Martin talked about the pressure on grandmothers and others when dads aren't in the picture. In my family seminars, dads frequently don't show up. In fact, of the single parents that come to the seminars, seven out of ten times it's the moms—and that's just my estimate. In addition to grandparents filling in for dads, I have seen aunts, uncles, brothers, sisters, and stepdads stepping in to help. The absent dad certainly has an impact on the family and extended family, not just the child.

The following real life stories demonstrate just how impactful the absent dad can be.

Kathy Stevenson

Kathy's dad, Colin, abandoned her when she was just eighteen months old. He also left behind Kathy's mom, Yvonne, and three of Yvonne's older children from a previous marriage, Sheri, Angie, and Greg. When Kathy was just six, Yvonne died of choriocarcinoma. Kathy's siblings were taken in by their father, Pete, after Yvonne's death. But he left Kathy behind.

Kathy was brought up by her grandmother, Elsie, and her aunt until she was fourteen when she moved from Florida to Oregon where my wife Sherry and I became her legal guardians. My wife is Yvonne's younger half-sister. We raised Kathy until she was eighteen. For two years, we lived in Oregon and then moved to Maryland where she graduated from high school. When the summer of her senior year was over, she moved from Maryland to Savannah, Georgia.

When Kathy got to Georgia, one of the first things Kathy did was start looking for her dad.

> *I don't remember much about my mom, just flashes. I do remember how much I loved her. I just adored my mom. I loved to follow her around and just be with her all the time. I remember moving in with my aunt Cindy when*

my mom first got sick. I remember the funeral and all. Years later, I was told my dad was at the funeral. I don't know if this was true, and I sure don't remember if he was there.

I remember Angie, Sheri, and Greg going off with their dad. It all didn't sink in at first. I thought their leaving was temporary. I just thought I'd be seeing my brother and sisters again.

The enormity of it all—my mom's death, my brother and sisters going away, having no dad, was lost on me at the time. It would be lost on any six-year-old. At six years old, I don't know if you can get your mind around death.

From what I knew of Elsie myself, and from what Sherry told me of her own childhood, I figured Elsie was tough on Kathy. Elise was sixty years old, and widowed. She had health problems—emphysema, among other ailments—and was just plain ornery.

Judging from my four years of experience with Kathy, I imagine she probably wasn't the easiest child to raise. She must have had acceptance and abandonment issues. My experience with kids with these issues is that they seek attention, both positive and negative, in any way they can. The attention they seek often tends to be negative.

I always thought Dad would come get me, especially when I was in trouble, getting punished or stressed out. I really believed this for many years. It took year after year of his not showing up before I let this go. I know it doesn't make any sense now as an adult. But during those hard times as a kid, I just kept hoping upon hope he would show up and take me away from everything.

I'm sure there were a lot of reasons for the call Sherry and

I got on a Tuesday in early December of 1983. Elsie asked Sherry if we would take Kathy in . . . permanently! I recall Sherry putting her hand over the receiver so that her mom couldn't hear us talking. I got the impression that Sherry wanted me to make a decision on the spot. "Get off the phone, and we'll talk about it," I'd said.

We talked about it, all right, and just four days later we were at the Portland airport picking up Kathy. In the four years Kathy lived with us, I don't remember ever asking her about her early childhood or her parents. I do remember that when Kathy neared her eighteenth birthday, she expressed interest in finding her dad. I couldn't believe it and spent some time trying to convince her otherwise—to no avail, of course. That's the power of Dad.

I never felt like Kathy's stepdad, or even a substitute dad. I felt I was obligated to take Kathy. She was family, Sherry's deceased sister's daughter. There was no question we would step up and take her in. I often said having Kathy was practice for when my kids became teenagers. But I still think I held back in being there emotionally as a dad for her.

Kathy describes her time with Sherry and me in the most upbeat and positive manner. I remember these times as being rocky more frequently than I'd like. When I told Sherry about Kathy's rosy outlook on her time with us, Sherry suggested that perhaps her time with us was great compared to her time in Florida. She had a loving aunt and uncle. She had two cousins and a stable household.

Kathy said she used two organizations to find her dad: Adoptee Search Organization and Finders of Lost Parents.

It was actually easier for these organizations to help me, because I wasn't actually adopted. And I do remember that they found my dad without charging me any money.

When I called him the first time, he was surprised, maybe somewhat reluctant to talk. We actually met once in Melbourne, Florida. He flew up in a private plane from Cape Coral. But the visit was stilted.

We talked a few times after that, but I could feel the phoniness in his voice. Once when I had a little too much to drink, I called him. That's when the hard questions would come. But he never came clean. He just said he and my mom didn't get along. Not getting along with the mother of your children is no excuse to abandon your child. And it is certainly no excuse to turn your back on your child when the mother is deceased.

Another time I was in real need of some monetary help, I called him. His response said it all: he refused.

Then when I was twenty-eight and had two little girls of my own, he called. I got to thinking: he left me when I was eighteen months, I found him when I was eighteen, and now he calls me when I'm twenty-eight; hmm.

I actually thought he was drunk, he sounded so bad. He was desperate to see me and my two girls. Turns out he had terminal brain cancer, and he knew he was going to die soon. His whole attitude towards me changed. My very first thought was, Well, fuuck you! I didn't say it, but it was sure ringing in my head pretty loud. I also thought, You SOB, you ignore me all your life and now that you are about to die you want to see me. But I let him say his peace.

Then I let my spiritual side take over. And I am glad I did. Because if I ever did something wrong, I would want to get the chance to be forgiven. I knew I would meet my maker some day. That's the part that won.

Colin invited me to a big family reunion around Thanksgiving, and I accepted. He must have called every couple of days to check in, to verify that I was coming and that I was bringing my girls. He kept asking to see if I had made my travel arrangements. He really seemed frantic.

Life, if nothing else, is ironic. Eleven days before the reunion, he died, and I didn't go to the reunion.

Six years after his death, I called his mother, my grandmother. You know what the first words out her mouth were? "How did you get my number?!" I guess I was just not destined to get to have the kind of grandmother that made chocolate chip cookies!

I asked Kathy if she had any negative beliefs about men in general as a result of her dad not being in her life. "Not really," she said. "But I certainly had some negative beliefs about men as a result of J. R. walking out on me."

J. R. was Kathy's second husband and the father of Kathy's second child, Kari. J. R. also adopted Kathy's first daughter, Kayla. Kathy and J. R. were married for three years. They were just friends at first. Then one night, Kathy had J. R. over for dinner. He stayed the night and just never left.

After a while we just thought, We might as well just get married. There wasn't a whole lot of romance to it! The attraction to a man that was like my dad was subconscious. It might have been a matter of convenience, or the fact I didn't want to be alone. I'm not sure.

Kathy said she married her dad when she married J. R. He was twenty years older than Kathy, and he drank. Then, one day, he just left. Not only did he leave, he took everything from her—including everything in her bank accounts. J. R. hasn't laid an eye on his daughter since. According to Kathy, "She wouldn't recognize her dad if he walked up to her and slapped her in the face."

When I was interviewing Kathy, I asked why, after eighteen years, she wanted to seek out her dad. "For me, it was a matter of curiosity. I wanted to know who my dad was. What was my history? Who are my relatives?"

Kathy expressed a number of feelings and thoughts that I have heard teens express over and over in my seminars:

> *Kids hold a universal truth: it's a given that your parents love you. Even when he didn't whisk me off on his white horse, there was still a part of me that thought he would, even at that age.*
>
> *My dad has to love me; it's the law. I had to find out the hard way that wasn't true.*
>
> *He discarded me as if I didn't exist!*
>
> *Today, my daughters have an awesome stepfather that has been there for them for ten years. I feel fortunate to have broken the cycle and found a man that loves and adores me and my children and who doesn't leave when the going gets tough. I feel very blessed for my children to have a "real father."*

Kathy's story demonstrates what I said earlier about this attraction—illogical as it may seem—that kids have for their dads. I didn't understand Kathy's need to find her dad. In my seminars, I was at first surprised at the number of kids who wanted to seek out their absent dads. But I have seen it enough to realize that there is an attraction, a bond, between a child and his or her dad that cannot be broken, even when the two have had no contact for eighteen years. The shame of it is that this attraction, this bond, is all too often one-way, from child to dad. If only the bond from dad to child had one-tenth of the strength, the intensity, and the passion that it has from child to dad!

The next two stories are also about dads who left their family, but these two dads didn't walk out like Kathy's dad; these two dads left very suddenly and unexpectedly. But notice the effect on their sons. Like Kathy, the two men were affected for a lifetime as a result of losing their dads at an early age.

Bill Ogle

As I was putting stories together for this book, I heard Bill being interviewed on NPR about his dad. In the few short moments I heard Bill, I could hear in his voice how much losing his dad affected him. What this story also demonstrates is the range of responses people have when being brought up without a dad. Earlier I stated many teens I worked with got angry. Bill admitted he was angry as a teen and afraid of commitment as a young adult. But once he became a father and just started being a dad it all fell into place.

Here's Bill's story:

> On a bright and clear August day, my dad, after kissing his girlfriend goodbye, climbed into the cockpit of his plane and headed East, an easy two-hour flight from Oakland, California to Reno, Nevada. We never saw him again. He left behind his business interest, a pregnant girlfriend, and three children. I was five at the time.
>
> When someone dies, even if it's suddenly, a series of predictable events are initiated. When someone

disappears, you're left with a void and an unknown. My mom, who had to take care of my sister and I, was left destitute, with the promise of alimony and child support gone. We went from a comfortable middle class life to welfare and food stamps.

Forty-two years later, on another bright and clear day, this time in September, a man, Steve Fossett—businessman, aviator, sailor and adventurer, kissed his wife goodbye, climbed into the cockpit of a borrowed plane, and headed south and disappeared. The subsequent search for Steve Fossett discovered what were thought to be undiscovered wrecks. These wrecks raised questions and possibilities about where and what happened to my dad.

I only have a few photos of my dad, a couple of portraits and one fading Polaroid of me sitting on his lap in my mom's apartment, taken shortly after they had separated. My Aunt Suzy, my brother's sister, emailed me about undiscovered plane wrecks being found in the Nevada desert. I pulled out the old papers and pictures I had of my dad. I hadn't looked at these items for years—his discharge papers, his social security card, and a few photos. After spending some time thinking about him and our lost relationship, I decided to contact the Nevada Civil Air Patrol to try and find out if any of the unidentified wrecks may have been my dad's. While waiting to hear from them, I spent a lot of time looking at the picture of me sitting on his lap and thinking about what I remembered of my dad. I realized that it was as much a picture of me and my son as of my dad and me. The same deadpan expression my son has when I tease him, the same crooked smile I get when I'm getting ready to poke him in the ribs.

My mom was very bitter over the divorce and my father's disappearance. It didn't help matters that the divorce was final the day he disappeared. She always said he did it to spite her, and I can't remember her ever saying anything good about him. She carries a deep and bitter disappointment to this day. I never shared these feelings and sentiments. That seems odd to me. I wonder why I don't share that bitterness, and I think I've begun to realize why I don't. I remember very little of my father, just bits and pieces. I've always had the feeling he would eventually return. These feelings turned to anger as a teenager and later, in my twenties, to the acceptance that he was gone. But there has always been the feeling that I would like to see him again.

After my dad disappeared, my second grade teacher complained to my mom that I spent too much time looking out the windows of the classroom and not paying attention to the lessons. When my mom asked me why I looked out the window so much, I said I was looking for my dad's plane. I was told he took off in his plane and never came back down. I just thought he was still flying around, not knowing that airplanes had a finite ability to stay aloft and would have to land eventually.

What I do remember of my dad has left lasting impressions. I remember sitting on his lap and him letting me steer his big green Cadillac. I remember going into a bar, a real bar, and sitting at the bar on a bar stool and drinking a Roy Roger. I remember flying in his plane and him letting me hold the wheel. These are the few memories I have of my dad.

When my son was four, my wife and I stayed at a friend's hunting cabin. This cabin was a ten-mile drive over private roads. When we pulled onto private land, I pulled my son out of his car seat into my lap and let him hang onto the wheel. I did this because I wanted him to have the same sort of memory of me that I had of my dad. I also let him drive the lawn tractor, me running alongside, and climb on the roof with me to clear branches and leaves after a storm. I've even let him back my car down the driveway, and I just bought him a BB gun. So, by modern standards, I may risk losing my son to government care—is that an oxymoron or what!— for endangering his life. We may have hit a tree on our rural drive, and he would be crushed by the airbag. He could fall under the wheels of the tractor or into the spinning blades. Not to mention falling off the roof or backing through the neighbors' house. Why do I let my seven-year-old do these things? I would call these moments with my son extraordinary events, or I hope they are, given the huge sensory overload that modern children are subject to. I want him to have lasting memories of me just in case.

My wife and I used to argue about the appropriate time to have a kid, but once the baby was on the way, I realized that being a father was something that was very important to me. I felt that it would fill a void in my heart, and it has. The most significant and important thing I've ever done was to have a child and be a father. Compared to that, everything and anything else is trivial.

My son was born at home in the back bedroom of a ramshackle California bungalow in a war-torn neighborhood in Oakland, California, a few miles from where my dad had last set foot on this earth. The experience of taking care of my son greatly increased my appreciation for my mom and the amazing amount of hard work that raising three kids by herself must have been. In fact, I think every single parent out there is a hero deserving of a medal.

I also realized I knew almost nothing about being a dad. I know what it's like not to have a dad, and I grew up longing for that sense and feeling of completeness that I thought a father or father figure would bring to our family life and my life.

At one time, I dated a co-worker, a single mom who had a little girl about five years old. I remember the way her daughter interacted with me, exhibiting hope and an eagerness for a male presence. I knew what she felt, and it scared me at the time—it reminded me of what I felt, wanted, and needed. The relationship didn't last long, my unwillingness to continue it partly because of being scared of the needs of a little girl wanting a father, but mainly because I was afraid of those feelings in myself. I've seen that hope in other children. The need they exhibit breaks my heart and still scares me, scares me because I realize how important I am at that moment to that child. I want to fill that void, heal their heart, and complete their world, a small and very great task at the same time.

What have I learned about being a father? Babies cry for a reason, not just to mess with your mind, I think. They can be pretty smart and pretty stubborn. One very, very long Saturday afternoon, I was taking care of my son. He was a toddler and didn't really speak. He wouldn't stop crying; nothing I did would appease him.

His diaper was dry and he had stuff to drink. So I finally said, "I don't know what you want, and I give up." I then took the daddy position (lying on the couch). He then picked up one of his picture books and brought it over, opened it, and pointed to a picture of a baby in a high chair. I asked him if he was hungry, he nodded, I fed him, and he stopped crying. They always cry for a reason, and they can be amazingly smart.

They grow, and they change so fast. My son learned to ride his bike in the street in front of our house with my wife or me holding and running behind him. The day finally came when he was ready and asked for the training wheels to come off. We rode round and round our neighborhood and when we got tired (the adults), he rode back and forth in front of the house until the sun was setting and we made him come inside.

I remember the first time I learned to ride a bike. It was on a bike that was too big, a single-speed with gearing way too high for a kid. We had a reasonably long driveway, maybe fifty feet. I had finally decided I had to learn to ride—the other kids in the neighborhood could all ride, and I was determined to learn. Back and forth, struggling to get up and get pedaling, falling, and even getting scraped up pretty bad. That made me stop for awhile, but the summers are long when you're young. I remember the afternoon that I was finally able to do it, and the joy and the feeling of freedom of being able to ride. I also remember that a flat tire meant weeks where the bike was not ride-able and the hills, which I couldn't ride up, where my friends could.

I watch my son ride back and forth and I'm glad that

I'm there for him. To fill his tires with air, adjust his seat, and run holding him till he could ride on his own. These are moments to live for where your heart fills with joy and sadness that they grow so fast.

My father is gone, and I miss him. I never got to say goodbye. I know and have known for a long time not to take life for granted. Every morning, I say goodbye to my son and give him a hug. Because I know, even though it's unlikely, it may be the last time I see him. At one time when I felt I had accomplished something with my life, I realized with great sadness that I would have liked to show my dad that I turned out all right. I know my mom is proud of me and that brings me much happiness.

I had five short years with my dad. It wasn't enough, but I think it had a strong influence on my life. I feel that I spent a good portion of my early life rebelling against him, out of anger at him leaving. I know I'm a lot like him. I can't help coming to the conclusion that those five years helped define who I became. Which tells me that every moment I spend with my son will influence who he is and the person he will become.

Because of an aviator lost in the same desert waste that holds the remains of my father, I had to revisit my distant past. I miss my dad, and I now believe he would have been there for his children. I wonder how different I would be, and if I would have ended up in the same place. Probably not. Finally, from the judge's statement on declaring my father dead nine years after he disappeared: "Other factors of importance . . . , including his past dedication to his children . . . which kept him in regular contact with them." Reinforces my belief that I would have definitely seen more of him. I miss him and know that every moment with my son is important. When I'm tired after a long day and just want to lie on the couch and my son shouts, "Dad, come and look at this!" I roll off and look, every time.

I noticed that Bill said he knew almost nothing about being a dad. He didn't know if he could be a dad, given he had no model growing up. He wasn't sure what the right thing to do was. When Bill just started being a dad, what he needed to do just fell into place. First, Bill wanted his son to have lasting memories of him. That realization led to little things like riding with dad on the mower and steering the car. Then Bill realized that "every moment I spend with my son will influence who he is and the person he will become." For Bill, this realization changed his entire relationship with his son.

Embedded in Bill's story is a case for how strongly young children want a male influence in their lives, like the five-year-old daughter of a co-worker Bill dated. And this hope and eagerness scared Bill. I think it scares a lot of men.

In the short moments of the NPR interview, I could hear Bill's voice quiver and crack when he realized the mystery of his father's disappearance might be solved after forty-two years of wondering. The audio is very touching. You can hear the story and the interview I initially heard at the following links: http://www.npr.org/templates/story/story.php?storyId=14330134 (Gonzales)

Or you can find it at my Web site: www.bobhazleton.com.

A CBS interview can be found at this link: http://www.cbsnews.com/stories/2007/10/07/eveningnews/main3340195.shtml (Blackstone)

Unfortunately, none of the airplane wrecks identified was

linked to Bill Ogle's dad, so Bill goes on without really having closure about what happened to his dad.

Rick Brand

I met Rick just after Sherry and I moved to Oregon in 1980. Actually, Sherry met Rick's wife Deb at a "Living and Learning with Your Toddler" class at the local community college. Soon we were socializing with the Brands, and we didn't stop. We have had Thanksgiving dinner with the Brands every year since 1980, except between 1985 and 1988, when Sherry and I moved back to Maryland.

One of my first experiences of Rick was his incredible appetite. We had Rick and Deb over for dinner and Sherry fixed one of my favorite chicken dishes. I really liked to take cold leftovers to work for lunch. Well, Rick had seconds and thirds, and wiped out the entire chicken dish. In my joking, sarcastic way, I opened the refrigerator and asked Rick if he wanted to check the refrigerator for other leftovers.

Another early encounter we had was hiking at Silver Falls State Park, just west of Salem, Oregon. Rick and I carried our eighteen-month-old kids (Kristina and Keith) on our backs. The child back-carriers in those days were not built like the heavy-duty framed units they have today. Mine was a cloth thing that just dug into my shoulders and armpits, but I was determined not to put Keith down unless Rick put down Kristina. But Rick never gave in. What could have been a pleasant, beautiful hike turned into a battle of who could be tougher.

That day it was a draw, but Rick is one tough guy. He got the name "Super Stud," and it fit. He biked to and from work every day for several years—that's not riding every once in a while. Biking was not just Rick's primary means of transportation; it was his *only* form of transportation. Commuting on a bike every day in Western Oregon is no easy task. It's in the dark, and it's usually wet from November through February. Rick is so tough that he even got himself home after suffering a minor stroke while he was jogging.

But as long as I have known Rick, I didn't really know much about his experience growing up. All I knew was that he was from Minnesota, that he grew up in Southern California, and that he didn't have a dad growing up. I didn't even know why his dad wasn't around.

Here's Rick's story:

I was born and spent my formative years in Southern Minnesota. My dad had a heart attack and died when I was three years old. I only have fleeting memories of him. Little did I know, even as I grew up, how much impact that would have on me when I became a dad. Don't get me wrong—my mom did a great job raising my older brother and I, but the father figure was missing in our life.

When I was reaching my teenage years, we were flooded out of our home. The situation was a tragic one for my mom as a single head of household. At that time, she met a man who helped us. After all those lonely years, he was what she needed. He turned out to be an alcoholic and was never the father my brother and I never had. He uprooted the family and took us to Iowa and California. The move was a culture shock for me and was very difficult for my mom as she tried to provide for us and reform an alcoholic man. He finally drank himself into oblivion. I don't know what ever happened to him.

Last I know he was in a mission. By then I had gradu-
ated from high school and was out on my own. I spent
a couple years in the Army with a tour of duty in Korea
before coming back and getting a degree in electronics
technology.

That's when I met my wife, Debbie. We married and
decided to raise a family in Oregon, where we still live
today. Our daughter, Kristina, was born first. That was
a special moment in my life that I'll always cherish. She
was born on my birthday and of course was my spe-
cial girl. A few years later came our son, Robert. He was
special, too, but in a different way. He was someone to
wrestle with, work with in the yard, and do those manly
things. We were very close as a family when the kids were
this age. We'd go camping in the summer and do other
activities every season. I helped coach Robert's baseball
and soccer teams and was a den leader in Cub Scouts.
Debbie was similarly active. I always worked hard, pro-
vided for my family economically. The Protestant work
ethic was one trait my mother instilled in me.

I recall working in the garden and having the kids out
there with me. I enjoyed working the soil and they found
things to do to with me. I think they especially liked har-
vest time. Fresh corn, tomatoes, berries. We grew our
own pumpkins for Halloween and carved them. We also
canned and froze a lot of the crop because we didn't
have a lot of money in those days and we liked know-
ing where the food came from. The kids were always a
part of that. Things seemed much simpler when the kids
were younger; or at least, we made them simpler. Look-
ing back, I think all things we did together helped mold

us as a family. I don't know that it was intentional, but the result supports our actions.

Even with all of this, I really didn't know how to be a dad, or so I thought. I told myself that story for many years. I kind of felt my way through it. Of course, being a man, I couldn't ask someone how to do it. As the kids became teenagers, I became preoccupied with my work and my soccer referee avocation. This was about the time my Robert was starting to head down a road that didn't support him. Of course, he didn't go down that road by himself. He brought the whole family with him. As I consider my absence today, I think that my time away from home during that time was, in a way, a means of escaping what was going on instead of attacking it head on. When I was doing these other things, I wasn't thinking about what was going on in the family. I used the rationale of doing to support my family, and I was supporting them economically. What I wasn't doing was supporting them emotionally or giving them the benefit of my leadership.

Family dynamics during this period of time were pretty fragmented. My wife and I went around and around with what to do about our son's behavior, seldom being in agreement. She was the one to be the hardliner, and I was the one to let things slide. What it was: she was the one who stood by her values while I put mine aside. It was only when we felt he had become a danger to himself and others that he went from getting our attention to us taking drastic action to save him. I was hesitant about giving advice or being tough on the kids. After all, I would have never considered doing anything maliciously when I was a kid, so why would my kids be any different? I thought they knew better and would eventually figure it out. I don't know that this had as much to do with my abilities as a dad as my mindset and confidence about being a dad. When I was in that mode, I was often present, but not available. In other words, I was there physically, but not there emotionally for the family. Looking back with what I know now, I see a lot of other choices for myself; but at that time in my life, there seemed to be only one way to do it.

I now thank my son for the gift he gave us. We chose a wonderful teen program for our son. It was one that realized the whole family is affected by these disturbances. The pain ripples throughout the entire family unit. As a result of my son's behavior, I took on a journey of self-discovery and self-healing that spanned several years and continues today. I learned a lot about myself and about being a dad. The biggest thing I learned was that I already knew how to be a dad. I just needed to open my eyes to what I already knew and to believe in my abilities.

I mentioned earlier that I was not one to communicate freely, especially about my feelings. Some may say that's a man thing, but I don't think it is, necessarily. After this all happened, I learned from my son that part of his rebellion was that he felt that he couldn't live up to our expectations. His sister did well in school, and he struggled. He felt that we wanted more for him than he could deliver, and so wondered why he should even try. This was an eye-opener for me. I had no clue that this was an issue with him. I had to ask myself: had I been more emotionally present, and if I had made more effort to communicate with him, would this still have been an issue? Maybe or maybe not. We'll never know if he would have chosen to share those feelings with me. What most amazed me was how unaware I was of his feelings. From what I know now, I would venture to say that if I had been open with my feelings with him and taught him that it was okay to express one's feelings, the result would have been different.

In this writing, I've focused a lot on my relationship with my son because he gave me more to learn about. I have to recognize Kristina for what she taught me. She gave me proof through the tough times that I wasn't a total screw-up as a dad. She stood by me and supported me as a dad. From her, I learned how to love myself and love my family.

I'll sum up some of my learning. By nature, we all know how to be dads. We have the ability to nurture our children if we only leave our egos and baggage at the door. It is important to have an understanding of one's personal and family values. While one's personal values are their own, a person should stand by them. When it comes to family values, it is up to the parents to agree on what those values are and to teach them through example and consistency to their children. I also learned that no matter how good a parent you are, that things still happen. That isn't an excuse to not do a good job being a parent. For me, (when negative things happen) it told me not to beat myself up for what I did or didn't do as a parent. As long as I took on parenthood with best *intentions, I shouldn't fault myself for my shortcomings. Nobody's perfect. What I do expect from myself is to learn from my mistakes. That's the same thing I expect of my children. Be in touch with your feelings and teach your kids to do the same. Really be there for your kids both physically and emotionally. Tell your kids you love them no matter what happens. They need to hear those words from you.*

I have two kids as different as apples and oranges, even though they lived in the same house with the same parents under the same rules. They each have their own identity, yet each is a part of me. I give them both my unconditional love as a dad.

Rick makes the point about the importance of being dad. He said, "I don't know that this had as much to do with my abilities as a dad, but more my mindset and confidence about being a dad." Exactly! It's not what you do, it's your attitude, your way of being a dad that is important.

Rick also said, "By nature, we all know how to be dads." It's about trusting yourself. I suspect Rick's lack of trust in himself as a dad had to do with the model he grew up with. First there was no dad, and then there was an alcoholic step-dad. Not an ideal situation.

Over the years, I saw Rick as a dad who took his job seriously and did a lot of things with Kristina and Robert. Kristina followed in Rick's footsteps in the electronics and video field. Kristina now works for the PAC-10 Conference in charge of video work. She gets to go to a lot of quality college sports events. I am seriously jealous of that. I also experienced Rick's hurt when his son Robert started going down a bad path. But Rick and Deb intervened in Robert's life, and they assisted Sherry and me when our son Jesse started going down a similarly destructive path.

Lessons

Both Rick and Bill offered up a number of lessons and patterns in sharing their stories.

Just like the kids in many of my seminars, Bill was angry as a teen because his dad wasn't there. Bill may not have been completely aware of the source of his anger, but it was there nonetheless. I got the sense that both Bill and Rick had an idealistic picture of how life would have been if dad had been there. I believe this idealistic view is formed when kids are just kids, three, four, and five. Then this view seems to get locked into their subconscious.

Because neither Bill nor Rick had a dad growing up, they didn't have a model to draw upon. Both initially thought they didn't know how to be a dad, but both these guys are just fine as dads. I believe it's a matter of trusting yourself, of going with your gut instinct. Sure, there are times when neither knew of the exact, right thing to do. But when they let go of doing the right thing and went with who they were and what they believed in, everything worked out fine.

Both Bill and Rick remembered the small stuff: sitting on Dad's lap, driving a tractor, being a soccer coach. Rick talked about camping, growing and picking fruits and vegetables. It's the small stuff kids remember. See Chapter Seven for more on how significant the small stuff is.

Rick touched on one of the most important things a dad can teach *and* live: values. I spend a great deal of time on knowing, living, and teaching values in the seminars. In

Chapter Ten, I will cover the importance of teaching values to your kids. Values are as important as anything a dad can teach his kids.

Rick also said, "I was often present, but not available." Boy, this is a big one for dads. How many of us bury ourselves in our work and then claim we are providing for our families? Rick said work and refereeing soccer became the places he retreated to when things were going badly. He rationalized that he was taking care of his family economically. I also buried myself in my avocation, football refereeing, and made myself unavailable to my family. But all our kids want from us is to spend some time with them.

Dads, do you get it? You matter to your kids!

–6–

Be Available

*We need [fathers] to realize that what makes you a man is not
the ability to have a child—it's the courage to raise one.*

BARACK OBAMA

OKAY, YOU HAVE decided to stick around and be a dad.
Great! One problem is that you will not get any credit
for having made that decision—at least not from your child.
Your child thinks you are *supposed* to stick around and be
their dad. Remember what my niece Kathy said in the previous chapter: "It's natural, parents are supposed to love their
child." That means sticking around. Besides, your child
will not (or at least shouldn't) know you considered bailing
on them.

In the previous chapter, Rick Brand said that after a while
he became unavailable to his son Robert. Have I ever heard
this time and again from kids in my seminars!

Putting work before family is far and away the biggest reason dads are not there for their kids. How about this quote:
"No one ever laid on their deathbed and wished they had
spent more time at work." Really! Yet I often hear dads say
that it is their job to provide for their families. Okay, I'll concede that rationale to a point. But just how much do you need
to provide monetarily? I've seen way too many well-to-do
dads—work-obsessed dads—not spend time with their kids.

But the excuses include sports, golf, fishing, you name it. I have also heard kids say their dad is off having affairs or getting married and divorced multiple times. The most destructive distractions are alcohol and drugs.

The two things I often put ahead of my family were work and football refereeing. I missed a lot of functions with my kids because of football. The worst was when Keith and Jesse were about eight and four and I missed trick-or-treating with them to referee a football game, a game I really didn't even want to work.

When the refereeing schedule came out in early September, I didn't have a game scheduled on Halloween. I thought, This is great! I get to go trick-or-treating with my boys. Then, a few days before Halloween, I was assigned a game and accepted it. I feared that if I turned the game down, the football commissioner would never again give me an assignment. So rather than go trick-or-treating, which I really liked, I refereed a football game. Another time, when Jesse was around six years old, I left his birthday party for a job interview with a company I didn't like and, frankly, wouldn't have ever worked for.

How many times have you dads refused to turn down work because you know or expect your family will understand?

All too often, I worked late or took on travel assignments rather than be with my kids. This set up a pattern that Sherry often pointed out to me. When my kids would ask if we could do something, my immediate response would be, "Sure, we'll do it tomorrow." But when tomorrow came, I had another excuse come up. Sherry let me know in no uncertain terms that I was just lying to my kids when I did this.

Let me illustrate how much kids want their dads to be available. My son, Jesse, lives in Corvallis within a few miles of Sherry and me. Jesse goes to college and works part-time, plus he has his own life. When I quit my engineering job and started facilitating seminars, I was gone from home a lot. During my first year of facilitating, I temporarily moved from Oregon to Utah. During this year, I was mostly out on the road and rarely in either Utah or Oregon.

Yet Jesse was much more bothered than Sherry about my long absences. Once while I was gone, he came over and repaired a toilet, then he sent me a text message that said he was now the "man of the house"! Here's the card he and Erin gave me on Father's Day 2008. Actually, I found the card in my room on July 1, after nineteen days on the road.

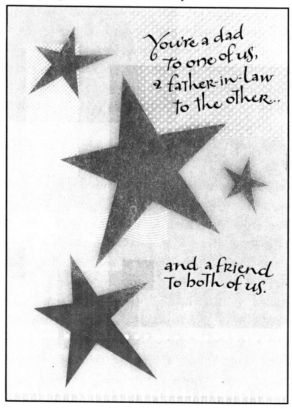

Happy Father's Day
to a dad
whose friendship
means so much.

Yeah when you're around!!

♡Erin + Jesse

Reproduced by Permission American Greetings Corporation © AGC, LLC

Notice Jesse's added note. Jesse just has this amazing ability to mask his feelings with humor and sarcasm. But I believe his point is he'd like his dad (me) to be around more. If this is how a twenty-five-year-old independent young man feels about having his dad available, imagine what it feels like for a young child.

I have heard all kinds of excuses for dads being unavailable. As I mentioned, the most common excuse is work: "I am supporting and providing for my family." Yes, to a point, but just how much "stuff" do you really need to provide for your kids? Check the upcoming chapter, "It's the Small Stuff"; you will hear over and over that the things kids want most from their dads is time and attention. Recall what Bill Ogle and Rick Brand said in the previous chapter about the small stuff.

Rick Brand said that his distraction was his soccer refereeing. Mine was work, travel, and football refereeing. I have heard stories about dads avoiding their kids by watching sports, whether it is baseball, basketball, football, or NASCAR. You should hear the excuses dads use during playoffs—the never-ending playoffs. "If they win today, they will force a game seven and then it's the conference semifinals." To the kids, it's not only another unimportant and meaningless game; it's also just another excuse not to spend time with them. I talked to the mother of a friend of mine about the sports distraction. She said her kids would stand in front of the TV and block Dad's view of the game, just so he would pay some attention to them.

I saw a girl in a seminar in tears saying, "He thinks going out and killing some animal is more important than going to his daughter's birthday party." Yikes, talk about misplaced priorities. It's no wonder the state of Illinois is withholding hunting licenses until deadbeat dads pay back child support. The state knows that there are many dads who put hunting higher on the priority scale than spending time with their own children.

What are the consequences of having a father who isn't there for his children? I've talked with girls who go out looking for the love and affection of boys—any boy. Some of these girls go down in a spiral of abuse. Their rationale is, "Well, at least he's paying attention to me." Other girls use Dad as a model of a man to avoid when dating and looking for someone to marry.

I've seen and heard of children who just want to get away from Dad as soon as they can. Some wait until they are eighteen and graduate from high school. Others find ways to leave home even earlier.

Some children withdraw from their dads and never have a close relationship with Dad. Some, as I mentioned earlier, decide they will be nothing like their dads. But Dad may have actually had some good qualities.

But far and away the biggest consequence is the long-term resentment some people carry around. It's hard work being angry at someone for a long time.

It's a shame that so many dads learn the lesson that they should have spent more time with their family *after* their kids have grown. Take Joe Gibbs, the Washington Redskins head coach and NASCAR owner, for example. From 1964 until 1980, Joe was a college and NFL assistant football coach. From 1981 to 1992, he was the Washington Redskins head coach. He returned to coach the Redskins from 2004 to 2008, but he left coaching after the 2008 season to be with his family after his grandson was diagnosed with leukemia.

Joe Gibb's work ethic as the Redskins coach was legendary. He would sleep overnight at the Redskins practice facility during the season. But when he left coaching for the second time, he said he missed seeing his boys grow up while he was coaching the Redskins the first time. He said he wouldn't do the same thing with his grandkids.

I've started to think that kids are more affected by having a dad who is there physically but not emotionally than by a dad who was never in their lives. At least you know where the totally absent dad stands. When kids can actually see their dads, they hold on to a hope that he will suddenly see the light and be with them. The disappointment for these kids is ongoing. Maybe Dad will finally show up for my game.

Maybe he will remember my birthday. Maybe he won't run off to work whenever the phone rings.

I used to work with a woman who had two kids. When she got divorced, her ex-husband moved out of state. He was rarely in his kids' lives. Randomly, he would show up and leave gifts, perhaps for a birthday or Christmas, but nothing regular. This woman said the kids would get all excited, and then Dad would disappear for months on end. Not a letter or phone call, nothing. She said she was left to clean up and deal with her kids' emotional disappointment. She said she would just as soon their dad never showed back up—it would be easier on both her and the kids.

Now, dads, I am not suggesting you quit your jobs, spend all your time with your kids, and become Mr. Moms—although there are dads who have taken this route. But I am saying: spend some time with your kids and give them the priority over work or your favorite activity. I heard of a guy who would make solid appointments for time with his kid. He actually entered his time with his child into his business appointment calendar. He didn't tell people the appointment was with his child. He just said he had a meeting at 4:00 PM. His appointment was to go to his son's game. The key is, he blocked out time specifically for his son; he made it a priority. For too many dads, time with their children is at the bottom of their priority list, or is not even a priority unless nothing else occupies their time.

Make sure your children see and feel that your time with them is valuable.

The time you spend with your children doesn't have to consist of big, extravagant events, either. For instance, my older son, Keith, remarked that we were one of the few families he knew of that ate dinner together nearly every night. It's so simple—twenty minutes of sitting down, having a meal together, and actually talking. To this day, Sherry insists that I not read the paper or mail or get on the cell phone or computer while we are having dinner together. It's about giving your children the idea that you see your time with them as important and valuable.

Jerry Green

I met Jerry in the year-long coaches' training I took in 2002 and 2003. Jerry is an extremely outgoing and caring person. He was involved in the program because of his relationship as a stepfather to a troubled teen. Jerry carried his learning from the program and the seminars into other parts of his life and is actively involved in coaching families.

> *I wanted to share my experience of my dad because I don't think fathers realize the impact they have on their sons and daughters by their tone of voice or the words that they use.*
>
> *My dad was not a bad or horrible dad by any means. My dad was a good guy—a nice guy. He was actually a nice, decent man. He just didn't seem to know how to show affection or to be vulnerable. My mom, his wife, committed suicide when I was just five, and I wonder if that event shut him down or if he feels guilty about her suicide. I don't know if he knew why she committed suicide, but he never shared that with me. I don't know if he was different before her suicide or if he was always the way I knew him. I don't know, but it seems like my dad just withdrew after my mom's suicide.*
>
> *I think I put up a wall about my life before my mom's suicide. I remember just flashes and bits of my early life. I think I just blocked it out. When I was about eight, my*

dad remarried a woman who had a girl and a boy, my stepbrother and stepsister. Then she and my dad had a child together, my half brother.

I can remember that—from the time I was about five years old—my dad never said much about how he was feeling about things or asked me and my siblings how we were feeling. He never talked about his life growing up, like growing up in Texas and what he did as a kid. I don't know if he played football or baseball in high school or college, if he had a dog or cat, if he liked to climb trees, loved art and theater, or any of the things you would think a dad would want to share with his children. I guess I really never thought about it much as I was growing up until I was out of high school.

My dad taught me a lot about mechanics, how to fix things. He modeled mechanics, not necessarily consciously teaching me. I kind of learned through osmosis, no conversations, no explaining.

My dad was a mechanic, and he could fix or build most anything. Even when he didn't know how to fix or build something, he did it anyway. The thing is, it seemed he didn't intentionally teach me about mechanical things. I don't recall him having a conversation with me about tools and stuff. I think I just followed him around and watched him. Or he might have asked me to get him a tool, and I watched him and then tried the tool myself.

When I had my son, I followed in my dad's model of not really being there and teaching my son. So guess what, my son followed my model of holding back. This is how the cycle goes; dad to son to grandson.

Once I was an adult, my family would all get together for an annual reunion at the river and ski boat and jet-

ski. But I didn't see my dad a lot between these reunions, maybe a time or two, Christmas and Thanksgiving. But there was not a lot of interaction between us otherwise.

My dad died when he was in his fifties. I went to see him in the hospital when it was clear he was dying. Although he was unconscious, I told him a lot of the things I wanted to tell him. I really thought I had made amends with him, even though he didn't respond. But when I got the call, I just broke down and sobbed uncontrollably for fifteen minutes or so. It just really hit me hard that he was really gone; I would never really know him.

After I took the program seminars, Discovery and Focus, I really came to grips with my part in the relationship with my dad. Not asking him, not pushing the issue, blaming him for lots of things and not taking it on myself. I didn't even feel the closeness to go and ask him the information that I wanted to know. On some level, I think I was angry at not having a father there to teach me and be close with me.

Fathers should model love to their kids—love and communication, express themselves. Dads, tell your kids how it was for you growing up as a child.

I feel like there is this big chunk of me missing because I don't know how he was raised or where he was raised and what kind of things he did as a kid and what he liked to do. There wasn't closeness. I am sure there were lots of occasions when we laughed and joked. But he was very reserved and quiet. There wasn't a lot of interaction between us.

Being a dad doesn't end when their children become adults. What I do with my son now—what I noticed I never did with him growing up—is share stories that relate to things we are doing. We will be out skiing and sitting on the chairlift. I will tell him that it reminds me of when I was a teenager skiing. Then I will tell him the whole story of how we hitchhiked to go skiing. My friend could drive his car to the base of the mountain, but his parents wouldn't let him drive up the mountain for fear he would have an accident. So we would park the car, get all of our stuff out, and hitchhike up to the ski area. So this is how I relate my childhood to my son. These were just tall tales about my childhood.

I realized that when my son got to be seventeen or eighteen years old, I modeled what my dad modeled for me. I was absent in that type of communication. I didn't know how important it was. I didn't know how to do it. I knew how to play with my kids, but I didn't know how to teach them, I didn't know how to have the conversation about "how can I help them learn?"

Consequently, I am seeing some of that play out with my grandson right now. What I am noticing is that the more conversations I have with my son about how important it is to model working behavior, and the more I talk to my daughter-in-law about it, and she talks to him about it, he is shifting into doing more things with his son.

In the last ten years, my son and I have become real close, and I am able to tell him all the things I have learned in my life, and especially all the things I have learned from the seminars I have taken. As I continue to learn and grow and realize what is important to me and what my values are, I talk to him about breaking the cycle. He's really a smart man. He's very curious about what I have been teaching. He gets it, yet it's hard, and maybe he's a little slow to implement it.

We are modeling all the time, whether we know it or not, whether we are conscious of it or not. Your kids watch you twenty-four/seven, year after year. Your kids know you better than you know yourself. If there's any truth to that at all, we as parents have to be mindful of how we come into the house, how we are with our children around our friends, how we are with them at dinner, how we are putting them to bed, how we are to each other. How do we talk to our wives, to our friends? The question is not "Can we protect our kids?" but "How are we going to live lives that will model a working way and a contributing way in the world that supports love and harmony—lives that they will automatically model?"

–7–

It's the Small Stuff

IN MY YEARS of working with troubled teens, I don't think I ever heard one kid complain that Dad didn't give her a car, or a cell phone, or a big birthday party, or vacation. What I did hear were kids saying, Dad never came to my games or Dad was more interested in his sports or hunting or drinking or drugs. I heard kids say they just wanted Dad to show affection, or to simply do one-on-one things with them.

While putting this book together, I asked friends and work colleagues to contribute personal stories.

Daniel Holmes on his step-granddad

Daniel Holmes, who also had a child in the program and became a seminar facilitator, agreed to provide a story. I had heard him talk about his difficult relationship with his dad, and I expected a story about how Daniel's dad wasn't a big part of his life. Instead, he wrote the following story about a simple chance encounter with his granddad.

> When I was young, my mom liked to visit her mom in Santa Cruz on the Pacific Coast. This was always wonderful. Going to Grandma's meant summertime, the beach, and, sometimes, our cousins. My two older sisters would take turns going to spend a weekend with Grandma

and Grandpa Nick all by themselves. I never wanted to. Grandma scared me, and I was always finding ways to annoy her—you know, mud on the shoes, dirty pants on the couch, and worms on the porch steps. But Mom was convinced this would be a great experience for me. Well, I can barely remember it, except for a few choice moments that were strong enough to grow on.

My Grandpa Nick was gone for most of the weekend. I don't know where he went or what he did. I made up that he wouldn't get in as much trouble with Grandma that way. I didn't know that he was my mom's stepdad, or that growing up with him was not very pleasant. I couldn't tell, because my mom was always loving and supportive with him. He never said much to me, and that was okay because it was a lot like my dad at home, only different. Instead of newspapers and chores and the TV, Grandpa Nick just wasn't there.

I spent most of the time outdoors looking at things that proved Grandpa had, at one time, been there. He had built the lattice patio, his workbench in the garage, and a huge greenhouse behind it. It was a pretty cool adventure for a young boy all by himself. His garage was full of rusty things: car parts, old paint, and dirty oil in old peach jars. It smelled dirty, musty, and cool. Grandpa Nick also liked plants, because there were hundreds of them in back in various stages of growth. It was neat to see what the baby plants were going to grow into. I was just about to pick up a watering can when I heard my grandma call. Uh-oh, maybe I spilled something in the garage, I thought.

When I got to the back porch steps, I saw Grandpa

Nick sitting on them. I thought I was in trouble and walked dutifully to my upcoming punishment. Grandpa Nick pulled out a pocketknife and opened it. My heart jumped. Then he picked up an apple, and I caught a fleeting wink from the corner of his wrinkled eye.

I sat down next to him, watching the knife cut into the apple. It was a short blade with a handle that looked like it was made from an oyster shell, except it was not rough; it was worn smooth over the years of use. His hands were old and leathery, like a fisherman's, but they were steady, confident. He would slice off the wedge and hold it against the knife with his thumb, bringing both to his mouth where the apple piece would disappear beneath the brown and white whiskers of his mustache. I had never seen anyone get a knife so close to their face before. I wasn't allowed to touch or use sharp knives at all, and I was afraid of them. So when he handed me my slice with his knife hand, I took it carefully, trying not to look afraid of his sharp blade. His eyes danced a bit at this, letting me know that he knew I was pretending to be brave and that it was okay. We didn't talk. We just sat there and ate the whole apple, slice by slice. When it was gone, he patted my head, and went somewhere, and I felt different, like we just did something very special.

Grandpa Nicholas Pastorino died not long after that, and then it was just my dad and me again as far as the boys in our family. Grandpa Nick was not my blood grandpa. My mom's real dad was an alcoholic and died in a park somewhere when she was young. My dad's dad drank himself to death when he was young too. Grandpa Nick was the only grandpa I had in this world, but that *was enough. There was just that moment on the porch together, but that was enough, too—enough for a lonely boy whose father was busy building his world; enough for an old man who shared what he could in the time that he had. Without words, without bloodlines, my grandpa and I shared a moment of unexpected specialness and belonging. Sharing life like this is what family is.*

While Daniel's experience wasn't with his dad, his story illustrates how starved kids are to have simple experiences with a male father figure. A couple of times in his story, Daniel implied or said directly that he wanted time with his dad. Just look at the simplicity of this story: a man eating an apple with a knife; a man sharing a few moments with a young boy. Nothing extravagant or pre-planned. Grandpa Nick was just being himself.

This little moment could not have been anticipated by Grandpa Nick. He probably could not have imagined that this silent encounter would have a lasting impression on Daniel. This is the difference between just being and trying to do stuff. Grandpa Nick, by being himself, created a moment when the opportunity presented itself. Can you imagine if Grandpa Nick had grabbed Daniel by the arm and announced, "We are going to go to the porch and eat an apple with my knife and create some lasting memories"? It would not have been the same. The moment just happened. It wasn't forced or scripted.

Yet, over and over again, I read about or hear of parents who go to great lengths and expense to create moments so that their kids will be happy.

In one of our seminars, we ask parents and kids to reflect on and share important events for their family since the teens were born. I instruct the families to draw a timeline showing the family highs and lows. Highs might be birthdays, a new job, moving to a new house, or a graduation. Lows might be a death in the family, a moving away from friends, or a bad vacation. After drawing the timeline, everyone in the family shares their timelines.

I have been shocked at the number of times that kids don't even mention the big gala events planned and put on by the parents. One example is that of a mom and her daughter and a sweet sixteen party. (I couldn't believe how many sweet sixteen party Web sites there are.) Mom remembers the party as weeks of stressful planning during which the daughter wanted everything just so. To Mom, this was a huge event, and from her perspective, not a pleasant experience. But Mom did it all because she thought the party was so important to her daughter.

The daughter? The party didn't even make it on her timeline. Mom was not happy that she went through all that effort, stress, and torment when she found out her daughter didn't think the party was worth mentioning.

Sara and her son

I was relating my book and the phenomena of parents throwing big parties for their kids to a work colleague, Sara. Sara had a son who spent fifty thousand dollars on his daughter's bat mitzvah. My colleague was just stunned when her son told her what it cost. Fifty grand on a party for a thirteen-year-old! What could Dad be thinking? Here's her story:

First, a little background. My mom moved to the United States from Europe. Her family members were strict Orthodox Jews from the old country. My dad was born in the United States, but his parents were from Poland. Just before my sixteenth birthday, my sister, who was just thirteen months older than me, got pregnant. The boy was Italian Catholic. At dinner one evening, she announced to the entire family that she was pregnant and either she had gotten married or was getting married.

From that moment on, my mom made my life hell. She didn't let me out of her sight. I could only see Jewish boys. By the time I was eighteen, I had been labeled and pummeled and punished. So the first nice Jewish boy I met, I married. We both knew we got married for the wrong reasons. In the brief time I was married, I knew I was way too immature. I also knew there was something wrong with this young man I married. I realized I was pregnant and my short marriage was falling apart. It was a long arduous process, but I gave my son up for adoption. He was adopted by a Jewish couple from Germany in their forties who had survived the Holocaust.

After his adoptive mom died, my son Josh found me and his birth dad. It was great to be reunited with my son and to see my grandchildren grow up. But I saw things Josh did for his children that just didn't sit well with me.

For his daughter, Ashley's birthday, my sister and I flew back from California back to New York. He had family and friends, and there must have been fifty people there. He had a woman dressed up as Barney and two others dressed up as Barney's cohorts. There was the cake and the food. For a one-year-old! I mean, the kid was dazed; she didn't know what was up. For Ashley's third birthday, Josh and his wife got a magician and a pony and more stuff.

When Ashley was ten, my son came to visit me. Josh and his wife promised her some foolishness. While here, Josh and his wife took Ashley to Nordstrom and let her buy a Louis Vuitton purse. For a ten-year-old! Just the idea that a ten-year-old had to have a Louis Vuitton purse is obscene.

One year I called Josh and asked what Ashley wanted for Hanukkah. My son told me she wanted an Ugg purse. So I went to Nordstrom and discovered that the cheapest Ugg purse was $130. I wasn't about to spend that kind of money on something that she would just discard in two weeks. Plus, I didn't want to promote that kind of foolishness. So I went downtown and bought a knockoff. What did my son do? He chastised me, of all things, for not buying an original.

I was invited to Ashley's bat mitzvah. That was a huge production. I stayed at my son's house for a week before this big shindig. After the religious ceremony, we all moved to a room for a reception. There was a photographer taking candid shots. There was another hired person with a video camera. There was someone airbrushing tee shirts. They had a DJ doing music. There was a cocktail hour with an open bar for the adults. After an hour and a half, we moved to another room for a sit-down dinner. My son spared no expense. The whole deal cost my son upwards of fifty thousand dollars.

Yet he could not afford so big a party. His business was way down because of the economy. It was credit card, credit card, credit card. I think what my son and his wife did was more for them. Yes, it was the religious right of passage for their daughter, but it was more for show. It seemed to me that he went to such an expense so that he could impress his friends, family, and the temple membership. It was like, "Look at what I can give my daughter." My son has a lot of good qualities, but he likes the attention. "Hey, look what I can do. Look what I have. Look at me." But when you are in hock up to your knees and more, I thought, it was the wrong thing to do at the time. But just what is he teaching his daughter?

I just think this overindulging, whether you have it or not, sets the kids up for failure.

My family moved to California when I was six and lived in a two-bedroom, one-bath apartment for ten years. If we were poor, we didn't know it. I was grateful to have hand-me-down clothes because I was fourth in line. I went to school and had meals, and I knew my parents loved me.

I worked hard for what I had. But I see a newer, younger group of parents that are able to give their children certain things. I think it's a greedy way to go, buying their kids off and not spending time with them, not giving them more tools to go through life with.

I have met so many people who just have their hands out, saying, "You owe me." I think you have to make things a little difficult so that children appreciate what they have.

By the time my granddaughter is sixteen, where is it going to end?

My son, I think, still harbors some negative energy that he was put up for adoption and that his dad is gay. I don't know if he's trying to make up to his kids for what he thinks happened to him.

At the start of this story I asked what must Dad be thinking spending fifty thousand dollars on his daughter's bat mitzvah. What do you think dads who spend this kind of money are really after? What was his purpose and intention? Was the party truly a gift to her? If so, how do you think it affected their relationship? Would your kids be appreciative or might your kids be like the girl who didn't even think to remember her sweet sixteen birthday party? Or perhaps as Sara said, her son threw the party to impress his friends and neighbors.

I have read a number of stories about similar excesses. On the CNN Web site on April 21, 2008, there was a headline: "$10,000 for child's birthday party?" As I went through the story, I read a story of a mom spending five thousand dollars on her three-year-old's birthday party. This three-year-old kid will never even remember that birthday party!

The article goes on to describe a dad who spent ten million dollars—yes, that's right, ten million dollars—on his daughter's bat mitzvah.

But starting so young with the lavish parties sets up a future where you have to outdo the last party. First the bar mitzvah or the sweet sixteen party is a big deal. Then the spring formal has to be a bigger deal. Then the high school prom has to be bigger than the spring formal, and the school graduation has to be bigger than that. It goes on and on until the wedding is just out of control. We're setting our kids up to keep expecting more and more from us.

Dads, what expectations about their relationships with boys are you setting up in your daughters with this kind of extravagance and overindulgence?

Cars

Buying teens cars really pushes my buttons. Perhaps this is because I was never given a car. Or it might be how many ungrateful teens I have experienced. If dads helped their kids buy a reasonable used car that would be one thing. But what I hear about way too often is parents agreeing to buy their kids a brand-new luxury car for little, if any, effort on the teen's part.

I saw parents use a new car as bribery. One couple offered their daughter a new convertible Mustang if she'd just complete high school. Completing high school is something the kids are supposed to do anyway! Giving the teen a twenty-five-thousand-dollar car for doing just the minimum is a bit much. Another dad pulled his son out of the program early and gave his son a BMW or Mercedes sports car in hopes that it would keep his son off of drugs. The car just made it easier for the kid to get around to his drug buddies.

One teen shared that his dad bought him a brand-new, fully loaded pickup truck. After a week, the son came into the house, tossed the keys on a table where Dad was sitting, and said, "I don't like it." The son proceeded to tell Dad about the SUV he now really wanted. Given that the son was in a program when he told me this, I trust Dad didn't get the new SUV for his son.

The flaw in this line of thinking is that bribery or enticement will motivate the teen to change his or her behavior. Instead, it only motivates the teen to do whatever it takes to get the car, and then he or she abandons the behavior. They have what they want, so there's no need (from the kid's perspective) to continue this so-called desirable behavior.

People tend to spend money on what they think is valuable. So dads, what is the value you receive when you spend big bucks on parties or cars for your children? Is the expense worth it? Is the relationship enhanced? Are there any lessons learned?

Here's an example of a program dad who assisted in getting his son a pickup truck—and created a big life lesson. Like many of the kids who come out of the program, Jim wanted a car to get around. He wanted to move over a hundred miles from home and go to school. So his dad, Doug, agreed to assist Jim in getting a used car. Doug agreed to loan Jim some money to purchase a used pickup truck. Jim and Doug agreed on a repayment plan. The plan included monthly payments to Dad, and included a stipulation that if a certain number of payments were missed, Doug would repossess the truck.

Watching Jim manage his money was difficult for Doug. He saw his son write checks for less than five dollars. Some of those checks bounced for lack of funds; then, the bank charged a fee of twenty dollars or more for the overdrawn check. So a check to get five dollars worth of gas ended up costing Jim twenty-five dollars. But Doug didn't nag Jim on the bounced check deal.

But when Jim missed three consecutive car payments, Doug, without anger, simply took the truck from Jim. Imagine: Doug taught his son a real life lesson! Doug set up a consequence just like what happens in real life.

So do teens really want and remember the parties, the big vacations, the cruises, or the cars? What do the teens recall as important times with their dads? It's the simple one-on-one times with dad. I just wonder whom the parents are putting these big events on for. Is it for the kid at all? Or is it for the parents, so that they can feel good about themselves? Is buying cars and putting on big parties a way to make up for not being in the lives of their teens?

Dads, what is the short-term payback for spending all this money on parties, cars, or electronics? What is your payoff? What do you get? What does your child get? Conversely, what are the long-term payoffs or consequences of giving these big material things to your children? Imagine the difference in the short- and long-term payoffs and consequences between Doug *repossessing* Jim's car and the dad who gave his son the loaded SUV. I'm sure it's hard on dads to teach their children tough lessons. But I believe the key is to look at the long-term consequences and lessons when it comes to giving money and materialistic things to your kids.

Jan Presley

Jan Presley is one of the longtime seminar facilitators that I worked with. Jan sent her daughter to the program and then got very involved in the program herself. She quit her job in the Bay Area, moved to Utah, and worked for one of the program schools. She has been a seminar facilitator for over ten years now. She has a great ability to be tough on the teens while being empathetic. I have found Jan to be very dedicated and committed to families, so much so that she started a group called Free Hugs for Us. (Check out her Web site at www.freehugs4us.org.) Funds are used to sponsor retreats, workshops, and seminars for individuals and families who could not otherwise afford to attend such events.

In one of the family seminars she conducts, she talks about how many families have dropped the little ceremonies or traditions. She stresses that having and keeping ceremonies is an important part of successful families.

Here is a story that she tells about a little family tradition:

My dad, Jim Presley, lived from March 20, 1930 to August 12, 2002, and left a huge footprint on the planet, especially with his family. He lived the value of service. His last twenty years were spent volunteering; in service to others, he impacted and inspired thousands of people and is well remembered across the country.

When he popped into the world, the first sound he heard was his mother's screams. She was unable to hold back her horror at the sight of her newborn son. He was born with a harelip and cleft pallet, and the treatment in 1930 was rudimentary surgery to close the gaping slash in his upper lip. There wasn't much they could do about the cleft pallet, and he lived with a severe speech impediment his entire life. As a kid, I thought it was weird that my friends couldn't understand him. Sounded fine to me!

My earliest memory of my dad is in a hospital. I was two and a half, and I remember sitting on his chest, my mom holding me still, a nurse, and lots of white—white sheets, white walls, white floors—tons of white. He was recovering from an accident on the job and had lost his right arm. I have no memory of him with both arms. I also have no memory of him talking, acting, or seeming like a victim of his circumstances. He worked hard. He played hard. And he is missed.

Our family had many traditions, some large and some small. For me, the most memorable traditions were the small ones: prayers before bed, getting tucked in at night, and family meals together nearly every night.

One of the most memorable traditions is still a topic of conversation when my brother, sister, and I get together. Every Sunday night after church, my dad drove us home using the same route. About a mile from the church was an intersection with a light. We knew if he turned right at the light, we were going home. If he turned left, though, we were going to A&W for root beer floats! I remember the three of us in the backseat elbowing each other, giggling, and whispering about which way he would turn. We learned early on not to ask or beg, because then for sure he would turn right. We couldn't see their faces, but my parents must have been stifling their own giggles listening to us.

I have been given an incredible gift in this life. I get to work with struggling teens and their families. Many of the young people I work with have lost someone close to them, most often suddenly and without notice. In the seminars and workshops I facilitate, teens deal not only with the hole in their life this loss has created, but also with the remorse and guilt for what was left unsaid in the relationship: for the "I love you" they wish they had said; for the hugs they wish they had given; for the hugs they wish they had accepted; for one more chance to say their true feelings.

In May of 2002, my father was diagnosed with cancer. Unlike so many others, I had the opportunity to tell him everything I wanted to say. He already knew what a huge influence he had been in my life, but I told him anyway. He already knew how much I loved and appreciated him, but I told him anyway. He already knew how much I admired his strength, his optimism, and the depth of his faith, but I told him anyway. And then I told him something he didn't know. I told him about the family seminars I facilitate. When I talk to teens and their parents about family ceremonies and traditions, I always tell the story of that very important intersection where the right turn meant home and the left turn meant A&W. He was surprised at the fact that I remembered that weekly game. And through the tears of our emotional sharing, we laughed and laughed and finally hugged. It was our last hug. It was the last time I saw him. I will always remember that conversation, that tradition, and that final hug.

Again, just notice the huge impact the little things in her childhood had on Jan. Besides the A&W weekly event, Jan talked about her dad's positive attitude, his strength, his dedication to service, and working and playing hard. I also notice Jan remembered her family's meals together nearly every night, much like my son Keith told me our family was one of the few he knew of that also ate together regularly. I keep saying this but, it's the small stuff.

My one-on-one time with my Dad

When I think about the pleasant and fun times with my dad, it takes me back to the years when I was between six and nine years old, living in Mount Clements, Michigan, and then on Selfridge Air Force Base. I recall going out on a frozen Lake Saint Claire one winter. I was just amazed that cars and pickups were parked out on the ice. I went around to the frozen-over fishing holes and tried to break the ice. Unfortunately, I successfully broke the ice and went up to my hip in ice-cold water.

I remember playing catch with Dad out back in this big, grassy area when we lived on base. I was getting ready for Little League tryouts. There were five kids in our family at the time, but there was Dad just with me teaching me how to play catch and play baseball. I also remember ending up flat on my back when I misjudged one of his fly balls, which ended up hitting my jaw instead of my glove.

I remember the thrill of Dad taking me—just me—to my first major league baseball game at old Tiger Stadium in a game against the visiting New York Yankees. I was one of five kids in the family at the time, but Dad only took me to the game.

Years later, I was reminded of another special memory of me and my dad. I'm not sure why the memory had been suppressed; perhaps it's because Dad and I fought so much, and because I was so angry as a teen. Whenever my business travels took me to Florida, I would visit my dad. When I happened to be visiting Dad on a Sunday, and I went to church with him, after the service was over, we were all invited to go to small discussion groups. In the discussion group, the moderator asked us to share our favorite breakfast experience. Say what? I initially thought. This is too weird! Who in the world has a favorite *breakfast* memory? But after an entire three or four seconds, a breakfast memory popped into my head—and it was a memory of just me and my dad.

When we lived in Mount Clements, we went to Saint Mary's Catholic Church. Every so often, there would be a father-son breakfast after Mass. When this moderator asked about our favorite breakfast memory, all the sights and sounds and smells of those father-son breakfasts came flooding back. I remember these long tables all set up with table service. I remember the white tablecloths, the glasses of orange juice, and, ooooh, the smell of bacon. It was just me and my dad. Mom must have gone home with the other kids. It felt very special for me to be with him alone, just one-on-one time with him.

If you noticed in Bill Ogle's and Rick Brand's stories, the fleeting memories they have of their dads were of these short, special, one-on-one times with their dads. I have heard the same thing from kids in my seminar: they just want one-on-one time with their dads. It really doesn't matter what they are doing—whatever dads do with their kids will be remembered as special times.

When my younger son Jesse came back to live with us after he had been in the program in Mexico for twenty-six months, one of the first things he asked about was when we would be going camping. Nothing complicated or extravagant, just tent camping.

When Keith and Jesse were kids (preteens), we would load up the van with camping gear, drive sixty to seventy miles up the South Santiam River, and camp with a couple of other families. Our favorite camping sites were Trout Creek and House Rock. We camped several times during the summer for probably ten years plus.

The boys and I would sleep on air mattresses in the tent with our dogs. Sherry would be sleeping comfortably in the van. Eating was one of the major activities. A big breakfast, sandwiches for lunch, followed by a big dinner. Dessert was (of course) s'mores over the campfire. The campfire was the central gathering place. Between meals, the kids would play in the river and perhaps even go fishing.

Sometimes the small stuff creates memories for us dads

too. One of my favorite camping memories was when Jesse was just a month old. For several years running, Sherry and I would take an extended weekend camping trip to Southern Oregon, to a small campground called Indian Mary on the Rogue River. When Jesse was just a month old, Sherry and I wondered if we should even make the trip that year. Sherry asked our family doctor what he thought of us camping with Jesse at such an early age. His thought was that there were probably fewer germs camping than at the mall. So off we went to Southern Oregon.

On one of the first nights, somewhere around 2:00 or 3:00 AM, I heard Sherry open the sliding door of the van; then I heard the tent being unzipped. She just thrust Jesse at me and said something like, "Take him before I #@$%^ him." I don't remember the exact word Sherry used; all I knew was that she was frustrated. Jesse had colic and never seemed to go more than a few minutes without crying. On top of that, Sherry has insomnia, and it had been just a month since she had delivered by C-section. I knew right then that I had Jesse for the rest of the night.

So I lay back down on my back and put Jesse on my chest. His head was just under my chin, and I cradled him with my hands cupped under his behind. I just loved holding him like that, so close. I could hear and feel him breathe. I could smell him and feel his hair on my chin. It wasn't often I was able to hold Jesse so close and still. Every time he cried or fussed, I just rocked him a couple of times with my hands and we made it through the night. Problem was, in the morning I had this tightness, as well as a lump, in my neck. It took half the day for my neck to get loose and back to normal. It was just a little thing. Jesse can't even remember it, but long after the pain in my neck and shoulders has gone away, I still fondly think of holding that small infant Jesse and rocking him to sleep.

During one of my many business trips, I heard a story from a dad about camping and the small events that make for lasting memories for him and his sons.

Standing in line to get rebooked (after yet another delay) on a flight from Phoenix back home to Portland, I was just fried. I'd been away from home for nineteen days. I'd run out of clean clothes, my mouth was funky, my feet were hot, and I was just plain grouchy and frustrated. I was standing behind an adult Boy Scout troop leader. I'd seen this large group of scouts for hours now, since we'd began waiting for our flight from Albuquerque. So I asked, "How many tickets do you need to get, ten?"

He said, "Twelve."

I just chuckled. "Like I've got problems. Where have you been?" I asked.

He mentioned some area north of Albuquerque. He then said, "We've been out on the trail for eleven days."

Again I laughed, this time louder. I realized I had been living in luxury for the past eleven days in comparison with that guy.

"I'm looking forward to going to sleep on a real bed, taking a shower, and using a flush toilet," he said.

"Ah, the simple pleasures," I responded. I told him I was writing a book about dads, and that, coincidentally, I'd been writing about camping on the flight from Albuquerque to Phoenix.

After sharing my thought that it's the simple things that matter to our kids, and not the big parties we throw for them, he relates to me a card he received on Father's Day in 2008 from his twenty-five-year-old son. His son brought up a trip he and his dad took twenty years earlier and how much fun it was. It was just a simple road trip, but for his son, it was a great memory of everyone in the car having silly nicknames and enjoying time with each other. The thing for this dad was that he hadn't thought of this trip in years. He may not have ever thought of it again, except that his son thanked him.

When children have grown up and look back at fond childhood memories, they don't remember the extravagant parties or the cars that were given to them. It's the small, special times that they remember. I have experienced this personally; I have heard it over and over from teens in my seminars: "We remember the small stuff." I also read one hundred and one such stories in *Chicken Soup for the Soul Our 101 Best Stories: The Wisdom of Fathers.*

I'm telling you dads, it's the small stuff that matters!

–8–

Teach Them Something

Children, just like dogs, need rules, boundaries, and limitations.
CESAR MILLAN, *The Dog Whisperer*

THIS ONE THING—giving kids clear, consistent boundaries, rules, and limitations—is something I saw missing way too often in my seminars. In so many seminars, I see dads wanting to be friends with their kids (you can wait until your children are in their twenties to be their friend) or dads just wanting their kids to like them, for their kids to think they are the *cool* dad. Some dads think that if they provide clear, consistent boundaries, they will have to be mean, or their kids will think they are mean.

The job of children, especially teens, is to push the boundaries, to find out where the boundaries are. So, Dad, it's your job to establish these boundaries, clearly and consistently, and to do so early on.

Remember Bill Ogle's story from Chapter Five? His dad went missing during a plane trip. Well, here's what Bill did to establish boundaries:

> There is a childrearing philosophy out there that is very
> popular with certain types of people. My wife is one of
> these people. This philosophy is spelled out in a book,
> which she gave me to read, which I did. Raising a child

is a challenge, and I am happy to have some sort of field manual.

I found this book horrifying—not in total, but in part—and especially in one area: letting the children determine their own bedtime. We have friends who followed this book, I think to the letter. Visiting them, staying late, and watching the kids getting more and more wound up with exhaustion, until they were literally bouncing off the walls, created in me an odd respect for the concept of bedtime.

Several nights a week, my wife was taking night classes. On one of those evenings, I decided that bedtime would be 8:30 with reading till 9:00, and then lights out. My son didn't object in the slightest. I should add that, up to this point, there was no regular bedtime; he went to bed when he decided to go to bed. After lights out, I sat and read in the living room until my wife came home. She came in and sat down, looked around, and asked, "Where's Jupiter?"

"Asleep," I said.

"This is nice," she replied. From that day on, he had a regular bedtime. A regular bedtime isn't for the kids—it's for us.

Remember, Bill said he "realized I knew almost nothing about being a dad." Yet he also said, "By far the most significant and important thing I have ever done was to have a child and be a father." Coming from this place of being, seeing fatherhood as such a significant and important thing, he knew in his gut a regular bedtime was important. Bill wasn't mean, he just knew the boundary of a regular bedtime worked—for his son, his wife, and for him.

Dads, I don't know if this is good or bad news, but your kids learn from you all the time. And they start learning from you from the moment they are born. Kids, whether they are toddlers or teens, are like sponges. They watch, they absorb, and they mimic.

Duane Smotherman, a fellow seminar facilitator, often tells a story of riding in his car with his then-two-year-old, Chase. Someone cut Duane off in traffic, and Duane yelled, giving the other driver a big, "Heyyyyy!" The next time Duane and Chase were in a car together and another driver came close to Duane's car, guess what? Chase yelled a big, "Heyyyyy!" Duane said he was shocked by how quickly his son picked up on his behavior and by how well his son mimicked him. Since our kids are always learning from us, let's be proactive about *and* conscious of it.

Duane got a real life lesson that children will mimic what we do. In teaching your kids; "action speak louder, much louder, than words." You have to model, that is, you must perform the behavior that you wish to teach your children.

Now just because you teach your child a value don't necessarily expect them to immediately change and thank you for being a wonderful father. Teaching will take some patience. The result may take a while to show up—sometimes a long while. But what I have found is no lesson is lost on your child.

Teaching a young child, full of curiosity, is a big responsibility. As dads, we have a lot of other responsibilities when it comes to raising kids. This responsibility changes as our children grow from infants to toddlers to teenagers. But ultimately, our kids become adults, leave the nest, and become members of society. That's why I believe our job as dads is to prepare our kids for the world. Yet what I consistently see in my seminars are kids who don't have a clue how the world works. So many teens want the privileges of an adult, but they don't want—and are certainly not being taught—the responsibility of being an adult. As I mentioned in Chapter Five, with every privilege comes responsibility. For the most part, the responsibility far outweighs the privilege.

Let's take driving a car as an example. I don't know how this started, but teens seem to think it is their God-given right to be able to drive at the age of sixteen—or sooner. But think of all that is involved in owning and driving a car. There is the cost of the vehicle to start with. Then there is the cost of operating the car: the insurance, registration, emission tests in some areas, maintenance, and fuel. All of these necessities come into play before you even get behind the wheel of the car. Once on the road, there are the uninsured and irresponsible drivers out there. There are also laws to obey. Getting a ticket is no picnic.

There was an incident a few years ago in Corvallis, Oregon that illustrates my point. A group of college students went partying and actually had a designated driver. But the designated driver decided to speed excessively. He lost control of the car, and people were killed. Does anyone really want to have that kind of responsibility? But it happens all the time. According to the American Academy of Pediatrics, highway crashes are the top cause of death for sixteen- to twenty-year-olds, killing about five thousand and five hundred and injuring four hundred and fifty thousand each year. (Committee on Injury, Violence, and Poison Prevention and Committee on Adolescence)

Many states now have specialized laws about teen driving. For instance, in some states, a teen with a driver's license may not drive with anyone under the age of twenty without an adult twenty-five years old or older in the car; they also may not drive between the hours of 11:00 PM and 5:00 AM for a year after receiving a license. States are taking action where parents and dads are not.

I read in the March 10, 2008 edition of *Time* magazine that only 20 percent of school systems offer driver's education, compared to 90 percent in the '80s. When I was in school in the '60s, I thought everyone took driver's education. More and more dads need to teach their kids about driving; not just about how to drive, but about the enormous responsibilities that come with having a driver's license.

When Jesse came back from the program in Mexico, I took him driving with his learner's permit. I wouldn't let Jesse start driving—he couldn't get in the car and turn the key—until he could perform some tasks related to the operation and maintenance of the car. I made him check the oil, the water, and the transmission fluid. He had to find the jack and the spare tire and show me how to use them. Simple stuff, but it showed him there is so much more to a car than just driving it.

How about cell phones? Once a luxury, kids now think they should have one by the time they are in the third grade. Teens these days must have the latest cool phone, and the cell companies are always making newer versions. Then there's the must-have ring tones, all for $0.99 to $2.50 a pop. Dads, you should hear the ring tone they have for you—police sirens or vulgar songs. Who pays for all this? You do! Every few months there seems to be a story of a kid who runs up an enormous texting bill. Dads, your children need to know cell phone service actually costs money—a lot of money if you are not careful.

I talked to a dad while shopping for clothes. He said if his son did not answer the cell phone when he called, the son lost the phone. It took just one missed call for the son to get the message.

My dad taught me a lesson about paying for phone calls when I was in college. I was twitterpated over a girlfriend, and every night I would come home from my moving and storage job (which paid $2.65 per hour) and have long, long-distance conversations with my girlfriend.

I clearly remember eating dinner one night and my dad giving me the phone bill. One month's worth of calls was $50.00! Bringing home maybe $2.00 per hour meant it took three full days to pay off the phone bill. I cut back the next month, big time, but I sure got real familiar with what long-distance phone calls cost, and I got very conscientious about how long I was on the phone with my girlfriend.

In addition to the teen seminars I conduct, I also do two seminars that both the teens and their parents attend. In one of these, we have a process in which we ask the teens to create a monthly budget. For most adults, this would be simple enough: what would it cost to survive for a month?

But teens frequently don't have a clue. They don't know simple stuff like tax withholding from paychecks, what FICA or Medicare is. The teens aren't aware that to rent an apartment or a house, there is a lot of up-front cash needed: first and last month's rent, a security deposit, and a cleaning deposit.

They sure know how to use a cell phone, but when it comes to knowing what cell phone bills are like, they are un-interested and out-of-touch. I have heard of cell phone bills in excess of five hundred dollars more than just a few times, and some of those were just due to texting. And why don't the teens know about what things cost? Two reasons: one is that we, as dads, don't teach them; the other is that we just give them the phone and don't let them know what things cost. Dads, I keep seeing this over and over: we give our kids things these days when they haven't earned the privilege. They would have a real clear idea of what things cost if we made them pay the bill.

But it is about so much more than cars and cell phones. I was talking to a young man and asked him what household chores he did at home. Incredibly, he said he never did any— *ever*. He said his parents had maids. I was dumfounded! I told him he'd better learn how to do some chores before he got married, and the girls in the training wholeheartedly agreed.

I see a lot of very successful parents in my trainings. They range from doctors and lawyers to engineers and business owners. Most of them started with little and paid for their own education. These parents worked hard, with grit and determination. And what do they do for their kids? They give. They just give them everything.

The teen's lesson? "I can get anything I want from my parents, and they don't expect me to do anything in return. If they don't give it to me when I ask, I can make them feel guilty, or I can whine, or I can get mad." And so many parents just give in. Parents learned so much by working hard and earning everything they have, but they don't allow their kids to learn the same lessons.

One dad in a seminar told me he wanted to give his kids everything he didn't have. I understand that urge. We dads don't want our kids to suffer. But by giving them stuff instead of teaching them to earn it, we teach them to be entitled instead of grateful. Dads, you do your kids no favors by just giving them all kinds of stuff. Sorry.

–9–

Teach your Children
about the World

I HAVE BEEN talking about teaching our kids how the world
works. What I have really been talking about is teaching
our kids how the outside world will directly interact with
them. I've mentioned cell phones and cars, and qualities like
hard work, determination, entitlement, and appreciation.
I haven't talked about how the world—the large world, the
global world we live in—works.

We live in a globalized world. Like it or not, resist it or
not, the world is becoming globalized. What happens in one
small corner of the world does affect us. Products and services can be manufactured and performed almost anywhere.

We also live in an ever-changing world, a world that
changes faster than any of us could have imagined when we
were teens. How and what do we teach our kids about the
world when we don't know what's going to be happening to
ourselves?

I see two things that dads can hang on to in this ever-
changing world we now live in. I described one of these
things in the previous chapter on *Being*: if you are solidly
grounded in who you really are, what goes on in the world
won't change you. Sure, you may dress differently than you

did years ago, and you may use a cell phone rather than a pay phone, but the person you truly are won't change.

The other thing that will assist you is knowing, declaring, and living your values. There is an upcoming chapter covering values. A solid value frame is something that will support you in spite of the changing world.

Thomas L. Friedman on Parenting

Thomas L. Friedman writes about parenting in a changing world in *The World is Flat: A Brief History of the Twenty-First Century.* In his book, Friedman talks about how the world is changing, shrinking. He also talks about the worldwide rise of the middle class, and about so many people having access to so much information through the Internet. As for parenting in the new flat world, Mr. Friedman proposes some radical ideas: working at getting a good education, tough love, taking on something hard, and personal responsibility:

> *No discussion of compassionate flatism would be complete without also discussing the need for improved parenting. Helping individuals adapt in a flat world is not only the job of governments and companies. It is also the job of parents. They too need to know in what world their kids are growing up and what it will take for them to survive. In short, we need a new generation of parents ready to administer tough love: There comes a time when you've got to put away the Game Boys, turn off the television, shut off the iPod, and get your kids down to work.*
>
> *The sense of entitlement, the sense that because we once dominated global commerce and geopolitics— and Olympic basketball—we always will, the sense that delayed gratification is a punishment worse that a*

spanking, the sense that our kids have to be swaddled in cotton wool so that nothing bad or disappointing or stressful ever happens to them at school, is quite simply, a growing cancer on American society. And if we don't start to reverse it, our kids are going to be in for a huge and socially disruptive shock from the flat world. While a different approach by politicians is necessary, it is not sufficient.

Shortly after this book came out my wife (a school-teacher) pointed out to me a letter to the editor in the *New York Times* (September 1, 2005) in response to a column on faltering American education by my colleague Bob Herbert. The letter summed up my feelings exactly: "To the Editor: Regarding the state of education in the United States, Bob Herbert writes, 'I respectfully suggest that we may be looking at a crisis here' . . . As a highly qualified teacher of English at the high school level, I agree. But this crisis we see in our schools has its roots in American homes, increasingly devoid of books and printed material, where children turn exclusively to television, computers, and electronic games for entertainment—and see the adults around them doing the same. Instant-gratification technology has, for many students, replaced the task—and the thrill—of reading. One cannot develop solid writing skills without first being a decent reader: underdevelopment of these skills translates to low scores in standardized testing across racial and economic lines in all areas. Education begins in a home where reading is intrinsically valuable and necessary; where recognition of the hard work associated with education and doing well in school are top priorities; and *where parents join school in having high expectations for their children's success. Without this initial foundation and continued support at home, a teacher's hands are tied at school. Jo Ann Price, Freehold, NJ."*

David Baltimore, the Nobel Prize-winning president of Caltech, knows what it takes to get your child ready to compete against the cream of the global crop. He told me that he is struck by the fact that almost all of the students who make it to Caltech, one of the best scientific universities in the world, come from public schools, not from private schools, that sometimes nurture a sense that just because you are there, you are special and entitled. "I look at the kids who come to Caltech, and they grew up in families that encouraged them to work hard and put off a little bit of gratification for the future and to understand that they need to hone their skills to play an important role in the world," Baltimore said. "I give parents enormous credit for this, because these kids are all coming from public schools that people are calling failures. Public education is producing these remarkable students—so it can be done. Their parents have nurtured them to make sure that they realize their potential. I think we need a revolution in this country when it comes to parenting around education."

Foreign-born parents, particularly from Asia and Eastern Europe, often seem to do this better. "About one-third of our students have an Asian background or are recent immigrants," said Baltimore. A significant majority of the students coming to Caltech in the engineering disciplines are foreign-born, and a large fraction of its current facility is foreign-born. "In biology, at the post-doc level, the dominance of Chinese students is overwhelming," he added. No wonder that at the big scientific conferences today, a majority of the research papers dealing with cutting-edge bioscience have at least one Chinese name on them. By the way, nearly 90 percent of the kids who go to MIT, a school like Caltech, also come from two-parent homes, where both parents can help guide a child down the straight and narrow.

In July 2004, comedian Bill Cosby used an appearance at Jesse Jackson's Rainbow/PUSH Coalition & Citizenship Education Fund's annual conference to upbraid African Americans for not teaching their children proper grammar and for black kids not striving to learn more themselves. Cosby had already declared, "Everybody knows it's important to speak English except these knuckleheads. You can't be a doctor with that kind of crap coming out of your mouth." Referring to African Americans who squandered their chances for a better life, Cosby told the Rainbow Coalition, "You've got to stop beating up your women because you can't find a job, because you didn't want to get an education and now you're [earning] minimum wage. You should have thought more of yourself when you were in high school, when you had an opportunity." When Cosby's remarks attracted a lot of criticism, Reverend Jackson defended him, arguing, "Bill is saying, let's fight the right fight. Let's level the playing field. Drunk people can't do that. Illiterate people can't do that."

That is right. Americans are the ones who increasingly need to level the playing field—not by pulling others down, not by feeling sorry for ourselves, but by lifting *ourselves up. But when it comes to doing that, Cosby was saying something that is important to black and white Americans, rich and poor. Education, whether it comes from parents or schools, has to be about more than cognitive skills. It also has to include character building. That is, parents and schools and cultures can and do shape people. The most important influence in my life, outside of my family, was my high school journalism teacher, Hattie M. Steinberg. She pounded the fundamentals of journalism into her students—not simply how to write a lead or accurately transcribe a quote but, more importantly, how to comport yourself in a professional way. She was nearing sixty at the time I had her as my teacher and high school newspaper adviser in the late 1960s. She was the polar opposite of "cool," but we hung around her classroom like it was a malt shop and she was Wolfman Jack. None of us could have articulated it then, but it was because we enjoyed being harangued by her, disciplined by her, and taught by her. I sit up straight just thinking about her! Our children will increasingly be competing head-to-head with Chinese, Indian, and Asian kids, whose parents have a lot more of Hattie's character-building approach than their own American parents. I am not suggesting that we militarize education, but I am suggesting that we do more to push our young people to go beyond their comfort zones, to do things right, and to be ready to suffer some short-run pain for longer-term gain.*

Unfortunately, it has been too long since America had a leader ready and willing to call on our nation to do something hard—to give something up, not to get something more, and to sacrifice for a great national cause in the future, rather than live for today. But maybe we also have the leaders we deserve—a perfect reflection of who we are and how we raise our own children. Paul A. Samuelson, Nobel Prize-winning economist from MIT whose textbooks have shaped economics students around the world for nearly five decades, gave a rare interview with the German weekly Der Spiegel, *for a special issue titled "Globalization: The New World" (December 2005). Asked what he saw as the future of the American economy, Samuelson answered, "We may still be the lead cyclist breaking the wind for the riders behind us, but the others are closing in. America's status as a leading nation is growing increasingly tenuous because we have become such a low-savings society. We are a society of me, me, me, and now—not thinking about others and tomorrow. I suppose the problem is the electorate, not its leaders. . . . In the past, bright kids who later became mathematicians were doing challenging puzzles. Today they watch TV. There are too many distractions, which is another reason we have this attitude of me, me, me and now." (394–398)*

Excerpt from "This Is Not A Test" from *The World is Flat: A Brief History of the Twenty-First Century.* [Updated and Expanded] [Further Updated and Expanded] by Thomas L. Friedman. Copyright © 2005, 2006, 2007 by Thomas L. Friedman. Reprinted by permission of Farrar, Straus and Giroux, LLC.

This attitude of "me, me, me, and now" is not just a teen phenomenon. If you take a look at the current financial shape of the country and the globalized world, much of it, in my opinion, is due to the gotta-have-it-now attitude of adults. No money down and 100 percent interest mortgages, credit card balances in the tens of thousands, eight-year car loans. These are just instruments of the gotta-have-it-now attitude. Dads, our kids watch our spending habits, and they think this is how it's supposed to be. The old adage, "Do as I say, not as I do" doesn't work. Remember, you are modeling behavior that your children pick up on. This behavior includes your spending and, hopefully, your saving habits.

When I wanted a new bike as a fourteen-year-old paperboy, I paid for it. I remember my dad driving me to collect from several of my newspaper customers so that I would have enough money to buy the bike.

When I bought my first new car (which, I'm embarrassed to say, was a 1971 Ford Pinto), we paid cash. I paid half and my dad paid half, but I paid my dad back within a year by making regular monthly payments. I learned about working for and saving for what I wanted. It never occurred to me to miss a car payment to my dad.

Friedman makes so many valuable points: the entitlement of American kids, the punishment of delayed gratification, the lack of emphasis on education, and the avoidance of hard work.

My parents grew up during the Great Depression of the 1930s. They are part of what Tom Brokaw calls the "Greatest Generation." I heard stories directly from them about what the Depression was like. My mom sometimes acted like she was still living in the Depression era. She saved and reused old clothes and food containers. She even mixed Pet powdered condensed milk with real milk to make the milk go farther with us six kids. It seems to me that teens these days don't have a clue about anything that happened before 1990. All these kids seem to be aware of is excess consumption and credit and immediate gratification. They don't get the idea of delaying gratification now for getting something you really want in the future.

I tell the kids in my seminars that the outside world does not care about them. The world will treat them as just another inexperienced teenager. The world will give them nothing, and they will have to work and battle to get anything. This is especially true in our current economic times, harder times than I have ever seen since I started being aware of the world in the 1950s. Dads, it's up to you to teach your kids about the cold, harsh world.

Sons and daughters

One thing that took me by surprise in my seminars is how teens of the opposite sex interact. What I am about to share certainly doesn't apply to all teens, but I see it in every seminar I do. Over and over, I hear the same story: boys mistreat girls, especially the girls who they claim are their girlfriends. They call their girlfriends vulgar and degrading names, they physically abuse them, they force sex on them, and then cheat on them. And girls actually put up with this crap.

So many times in a seminar, a girl stands up and shares something about her old boyfriend. I ask, "Just how did he treat you?"

The girl generally puts her head down, her voice lowers, and the answer is always the same: "He treated me badly," or "Like crap," or some similar description. Sometimes the girl says her boyfriend is "overprotective." When I ask what "overprotective" means, she says her boyfriend is always checking up on her. The boy doesn't allow her to have any friends. The boy gets angry when the girl does something, anything, without his knowledge.

Here's the clincher. When I ask, "How long did you stick

with him?" the answer from these fourteen-, fifteen-, and sixteen-year-old girls is in *years*, not months or weeks. These girls put up with this abuse for years! And so many times, the girls say they were just looking for some male companionship because Dad was not there to give them any love, affection, or attention. I really get on the girls. I tell them that the boys will keep up with crass behavior as long as there are girls who take it!

So, Dads, what can you do? Lots! Dads with sons: Teach your sons what treating females with respect looks like. You can certainly tell them, but showing them is so much more effective.

How do you treat women? How do you treat your wife? As I said, Dads, your sons are watching. What behaviors are you, as dads, modeling?

Now, Dads with daughters, there is an awful lot you can do, too. I tell girls not to put up with degrading, disrespectful boys. It is a fact that we, all of us, teach people how to treat us. So I tell the girls that they are the ones in control of how boys treat them. It is up to them to insist upon—to *demand*—dignity and respect.

So, Dads, what can you do? How about simply teaching your daughters to demand respect from boys. How do you treat your own daughter? How do you treat women in general, and your wife, and your child's mother? Just like boys, your daughters are watching and learning from you.

I mentioned this before: some girls have the rationale that "If my dad treats me poorly, then that's what's normal." Dads, disrespect is not normal. Teach them what respect looks like.

Values

IN THE PREVIOUS chapters I discussed and gave examples of teaching your kids how some things work . . . mechanically, electrically, electronically, and globally, that is. While it is great and important to know how new things work and how the new world works, we as a society have lost the connection to older, much more basic concepts.

You'll notice that as I moved through the previous chapter, I got into things that were bigger, broader. Respect, for example, is a bigger concept than what cell phones cost. This is because respect is a value. Dads, you can go a long way in raising responsible kids by teaching your children about values. In fact, if there is just one thing you teach your children, teach them about having and living their values.

Again, the best way to teach values is to consistently model living your values.

The term "value" is one of the words I use in my seminar whose definition is, frankly, warped by society—in the media and in general conversations. The terms "value" and "family values" are often used in a political context. I have seen bumper stickers that say "Hate Is Not a Family Value." To me, this bumper sticker is a response to a group's political stance. I even heard of a University of Michigan football player quitting the team because, as he said, the team did not support "family values"—whatever he meant by "family values."

I'd like you to put aside other definitions of values. The value definitions I will be using are *personal* values, *personal* choices that guide *personal* behavior.

The definition of values that I use in my seminars is: "the consciously chosen guiding principles that actively encompass every area of my life."

Although the definition is only thirteen words long, it can seem a bit unwieldy so let me break it down.

Consciously chosen. This simply means we make a conscious choice of our personal values from many alternatives. Not everyone has the same values. We all make personal choices about what values are important to us. The "consciously chosen" part is critical. Unlike many beliefs, especially beliefs we have about ourselves, values are consciously chosen. So many beliefs we have about ourselves are *not* consciously chosen. For example, in seminars, I'll ask someone, "Did you wake up one morning and say, 'You know, today I think I'll start believing that I am inadequate'?" The answer is always "No!" The belief was just there, as if it had always been there; it's in our subconscious. Values, however, are consciously, purposely chosen.

Guiding principle. The term "guiding principle" is like a guardrail on a curvy mountain road, or to the bumpers that are placed in the gutters on a bowling alley. Values, when lived, will keep you on the path and out of the ravine or the gutter. Values are big concepts—principles—not simply behaviors. For instance, "always telling the truth," in my opinion, is more like a specific behavior than a principle. Integrity, however, is a much bigger concept. Integrity covers much more than telling the truth. It is about saying what you do and doing what you say.

Actively encompass. This simply means that once a value is declared, it requires action. One of the core principles of the seminars I conduct is: "the universe rewards action, not just thinking." To me, this means that thinking is important, but that at some point, action is required. To have and live a value, certain behaviors are required. For example, an employee once told me he would give me at least two weeks notice when it came time for him to quit. But when he eventually did give notice, he gave me maybe eight days. When I reminded him about his promise to give me two weeks notice, he said, "I like to keep my word."

I said, "Well, you might like to keep your word, but right now you are not keeping your word." So living your values takes action, and sometimes that requires hard work and tough decisions. It's easy to live your values when the choices are easy.

I heard a well-known radio and television personality say that he believed sometimes people do have to compromise their values. Sorry, if you start compromising your values they are no longer values. They may be nice ideas, or beliefs, or ideals you sometimes strive for, but just don't call them values. They are not values if you discard them when things get difficult.

Every area of my life. There are two things to consider here. First, beliefs often only apply to certain areas of my life. I believe I am good at math; I believe Honda makes a reliable automobile—these are beliefs that apply to specific areas of my life. Second, a value will guide your choices in every area of your life. Honesty and integrity, if chosen as values, will apply at home, at work, during sports (including golf), while driving, when doing taxes—everywhere! You don't get to pick and choose where you apply these values. Otherwise, they are not really values.

I'd like to illustrate two concepts about values through a personal story about football and football refereeing. The concepts are: 1) values are not likes and dislikes, and 2) value-based choices, while they may not be easy, are simple.

I enjoy football and football refereeing. Football is certainly not a value. But often, I let my liking of football get in my way of my value of family. I started playing football when I was eleven and played through high school. Over the years, I have been a big football fan. I have refereed youth, high school, and college football. I'm embarrassed to say so, but Sherry and I scheduled our honeymoon so that I could be home for my first football referee meeting of the season back in 1976. Yikes! I wasn't exactly living my value of family at that point.

Remember my earlier story about football refereeing rather than taking my kids out on Halloween? I claimed I had a value called family at that time. Well, I wasn't living my value of family at that moment, was I? Many years later, I had a similar decision to make regarding football refereeing and my value of family. But the difference this time was that I had been to a number of seminars myself and done extensive values work.

My brother Pat called me and invited me to see his daughters in a violin concert on a Saturday evening. His daughters were eleven and fifteen at the time. Have you ever heard eleven-year-olds play the violin? It isn't necessarily all that good. What I had planned at that time was the post-game football get-together with the other referees. I agonized for a while. Then the lessons I learned from doing values work kicked in. I declared a value call: family. This included my brother and his family. So I made the arrangements to leave my football game as soon as it was over. This involved driving to the game separately and telling my fellow referees why I couldn't stay. I was afraid of what they would say, but they all really and truly understood. So again, the choice intellectually was simple: go to the concert. But I tried to make it hard. Why? Because I like football. Football refereeing may be something I like to do, but it is not a value.

As dads, our job around values is threefold. We must:

Know our values

Live our values

Teach our values

Knowing your values—really knowing your values—actually takes some work. It's not simply a case of saying, "Oh, my values are love, family, respect, and integrity." In my seminars, I use two separate, short exercises to illustrate values-based choices. I lecture for up to an hour on values. Then I assign homework: I instruct parents and teens to write down their values and describe what they look like. Once they've completed the assignment, I have parents and teens discuss and ask questions of each other about their values.

For the teens, we dedicate an entire day's seminar to teaching values. We do not teach them what values to have; rather, we teach the concept of values. In subsequent seminars, we ask teens to rate themselves on how they have been living their values.

We ask adults to take on a seven-week values workbook.

Seven weeks! One of the most interesting pieces of this work is to track your time for a week and then compare where you spend your time to what your values are. This process was an eye-opener for me. I spent the bulk of my time sleeping, being at work or coming and going from work, watching TV, exercising, or refereeing football. That didn't leave much time for family. But family was one of my declared values. Something had to give. Either I had to give up the idea that I had a value called "family," or I had to actually spend time with my family. I chose to spend more time with my family.

I didn't have to give up football refereeing or TV or exercising, but I started making family a priority. I decided that I didn't need to accept every single refereeing assignment given to me. When Keith started playing junior varsity football, I arranged my schedule so that I was free to see his games. I admittedly held back, sometimes showing up at halftime. When Keith and Jesse started wrestling, I cleared everything else from my schedule and went to their meets, long and boring as they might have been.

I remember an instance when I was able to model *knowing* and *living* my values. I missed the *teaching* part, though. At the age of five, Jesse came home from Brandon's house across the street with a five-dollar bill. When I asked Jesse about the money, he said he had found it at Brandon's. I'm not sure exactly what I said to Jesse, but it was probably something along the lines of, "Get your butt back over there and give the money back!" I knew my value and lived the value—I just didn't do such a good job teaching Jesse the value. A calm, quick little sit-down talk with Jesse would have been all that was needed.

It takes a little work to know what your values are. What I

experienced, both personally and in seminars, was that most people do not spend much if any time doing values work. We often spend more time planning vacations, talking about the Super Bowl, or tracking our NCAA basketball brackets than we do discussing values.

By doing values work, I mean *declaring* our values, *defining* the values, and *knowing* what living these values will look like. I have provided a link on my Web site (www.bobhazleton.com) to a downloadable values workbook. This is the seven-week workbook designed for you to declare, define, and clarify just what your values will look like.

I have heard from parents who have taken on the values workbook and included their preteens. These ten- and eleven-year-olds have really taken on the values work. I have heard that these preteens actually enjoyed being included in this work. I have even heard from parents that, when arguing starts up, the youngsters remind everyone in the family of the value of respect. The lesson? Teach your kids about values early on, and they will be more likely to embrace them—and, most important, *live* them. Then, when the tough decisions in the teen years come up, your kids will have a solid base of values to draw upon.

A few final thoughts on values:

- Parents, you and only you set the values for the family. You are the parents; it's your house! You can take input from your kids, but you are the authority at home.
- Values apply to everyone living in your house, including adult children *and* you. Don't make values just to stop some objectionable behavior or to control your children.
- Values create boundaries for both you and your children.

As the quote from Cesar Millan says at the start of this chapter, values will create rules, boundaries, and limitations. I don't know how this happens, but the job of teenagers is to test and find out where these boundaries are. It's your job, Dad, to let your teen know, very clearly, where these boundaries are.

• Values are not prioritized. That is, no one value is more important than any other. Prioritizing values creates excuses to avoid living the "lower" value.

Learn something from your children

Now, throughout the past two chapters, I talked about fathers teaching their kids. But let's not be so naive as to think that we can't learn, especially from our kids. Sure, my kids have taught me a lot about electronics and new technology—how to program a VCD or hook up the DVR or how to find out just what my cell phone can do—but I have learned some much bigger lessons from my two sons. Keith has taught me about hard work, passion, and endurance. To say Keith is an overachiever is a bit too simplistic. He got straight A's in high school, he went to the honors college at Oregon State University, and he is in an eight-year combined MD-PhD program in New York City.

But what I saw in him, just in his high school wrestling career, showed how much he made of his natural talents. Keith was not a natural athlete or a star wrestler. He started off with a slight handicap—he's missing one of his pectoral muscles. The doctor said a nerve might have gotten pinched when he was a child; we don't know exactly. But Keith didn't let that or anything else stop him.

What Keith may have lacked in natural ability, he made

up for in hard work and determination. Keith always showed up at the early-morning running sessions during the wrestling season. He always had a good attitude, even though he seemed to be wrestling behind really talented teammates. But Keith had a week in January of 1996 when it all came together. The Corvallis wrestling team had a tournament in Redmond, Oregon, about one hundred miles away from Corvallis. The top wrestler on the team was sick and couldn't make the trip, so Keith was able to wrestle in his preferred weight. He eventually won his weight class, winning one match (as he said), by holding on to an opponent's leg literally by a fingertip. At the next league match, the coach rewarded Keith's efforts by again letting him wrestle at his lower preferred weight, while the team's star wrestled up a weight class. Keith responded by winning that match in overtime. I see Keith as someone who never gives up. I sure could have used that determination when I was his age. Heck, I could use it now.

Jesse, on the other hand, taught me a few things about having fun and loosening up some. Both he and Keith think I'm so uptight that I seem to have a broomstick stuck somewhere in my body. You get the idea. Jesse was all about being carefree and having fun. For me, it was frustrating to watch him play sports as a kid. He just looked like he was out there messing around. But he sure surprised me in his first high school wrestling match as a freshman. "He pinned his guy!" I kept telling other parents. Jesse had actually paid attention all those years watching Keith wrestle. No matter what Jesse does, he finds some fun in it.

To this day, Jesse gets on me when I am too serious and when I don't want to do something different. Sometimes when I would just rather sit home and watch TV, he will come over and tell me we are going to do something. In the fall of 2008, Jesse insisted we go to an Oregon State football game versus Southern Cal. I figured the game would be sold out and the Beavers would get crushed. (USC was ranked number one in the country at the time, and Oregon State was just 1–2.) But Jesse wouldn't take no for an answer. So we walked to the game—a mile and a half away. Jesse had his student ticket so I bought a ticket from a scalper at a reduced price because the game wasn't sold out like I thought. Then we watched a fantastic game, which the Beavers won. After the game was over, we went onto the field, which was a mob scene. But if it had been up to me, I would have just sat at home.

Jesse also taught me about traditions. He insists we keep traditions alive. When he was in Mexico for two years in the program, Sherry and I just didn't have the energy or motivation to put up a Christmas tree. Jesse never allows that to happen when he is here. One year, Sherry had to work at the hospital on Christmas. So we decided to do our Christmas on Christmas Eve. Sherry went to work on Christmas while Keith, Jesse, and I went snow skiing. All day long, Jesse kept saying that it just wasn't right.

Jesse also showed me that people can change and mature. I frankly didn't like Jesse very much at the age of fifteen. There was a big portion of his eighteenth and nineteenth years I didn't like much either. He was doing drugs, he was dishonest, and he was defiant and angry. He didn't show much respect to me or to anyone with authority, and he wasn't the least bit honest. But now, he is a kind, sensitive, honest, and hardworking young man. One evening, he was over visiting when we told him about a negative prognosis for his aunt Jeanne, my brother Pat's wife. Jesse got emotional; he cried a little bit and said, "It just isn't fair." To think how insensitive Jesse was as a teen, and then to see that, was amazing.

Jesse has been working as a certified nurse's aide (CNA) for a number of years, with the goal of becoming a physician's assistant (PA) or a nurse. His work taking care of people's basic needs while they are in the hospital is a complete turnaround from his attitude as a teen. A fellow football referee was in the hospital with kidney stones and wrote this letter after Jesse was there for him:

> *Dear Bob and Sherry,*
>
> *Last week I had the misfortune of an attack of kidney stones with complications, so . . . I was admitted to Good Samaritan Hospital. Near the bottom of my downward spiral of discomfort and pain, an angel appeared at my bedside, and I want to tell you about him.*
>
> *He was friendly, kind, and compassionate. He had an attitude of responsibility with a bit of a "twinkle" in his eye. He was willing to talk with, but mostly listen to, an "old duffer" babble on. (I can talk a lot, but this was worse because by now I was pretty full of "joy juice.") During our several talks (he did have other things to do), I discovered he was a Hazleton and your son.*
>
> *I know of some of the agony and anguish you have experienced. However, I thought it important that you know of the young man I met. He was a son of whom anyone could be proud. He was bright, thoughtful, and caring. I was pleased to hear that he had life goals and that he saw himself with a real future.*
>
> *Thanks for not giving up on your son. I was glad he was there when I needed him—as you were for him.*
>
> *Wayne Fisk*

–11–

Communication

THIS IS OH-SO-SIMPLE. If you want to communicate—really communicate—with your kids, do the following simple things:

Sit down,
shut up,
and listen, really listen!

Turn off your cell phone, your pager, your Blackberry, your iPod, your computer, your TV, your music. Put down the newspaper, the sports page, the financial section, the vacation brochure, the magazine, and your work papers. Look your kids in the eye and listen to them. If your kids are small enough, put them on your lap and listen. Just listen. Do not offer advice. Do not try to fix anything. Just listen.

For most of us, this will take practice. You want to practice authentic listening. Authentic listening is simply listening without agenda, bias, or response. Let me break down each of these three words.

Without agenda. This means we put aside our wants, our needs, and what we believe to be important. We listen to the other person as if what they have to say is the most important thing in the world—because to them, it is the most important thing in the world at that particular moment.

Without bias. This means being impartial, having no judgment, having no prejudice. Even if you think what the other person is saying is silly, unimportant, or irrelevant.

Without response. In its simplest form, this simply means keeping your mouth shut. But this also means keeping your mind quiet. Keeping all of your suggestions not only to yourself, but also out of your mind. You are not to think of how to solve their problem. For guys, this can be tough. For some reason, guys have gotten the idea that their job is to solve problems, especially their kids' and their spouse's problems. I have to tell you, guys, most people just want to be sure you are listening to them.

Here's how Morrie Schwartz, of *Tuesdays with Morrie*, described listening authentically:

> *"I believe in being fully present," Morrie said. "That means you should be with the person you are with. When I'm talking to you now, Mitch, I try to keep focused on only what is going on between us. I am not thinking about something we said last week. I am not thinking of what's coming up this Friday. I am not thinking about doing another Koppel show or about what medications I'm taking.*
>
> *"I am talking to you. I am thinking about you." (Albom 135–136)*

Again, we dads seem to have this need to make our point in conversations. The beauty of authentic listening is that our point *will* come out. It will come out in the flow of the conversation, not because we rammed it into the conversation in our impatience.

In the parent-child seminars I do, dads seem to have trouble with this being silent/authentic listening concept. During family sharing time, I often ask each family member to share, *uninterrupted*, for four minutes. Four lousy minutes! And my biggest task during these four minutes is to get family members to honor each other's four minutes. The biggest culprits during these sharing periods seem to be the dads. It's as if we dads are born with the need to fix others' problems, but rarely do our kids want this. Just listen until they ask you otherwise.

Later in this chapter, I'll going to give a couple of listening techniques and some book references. However, all these techniques are useless if your kids think that you don't care or that you aren't actually listening. *Act like you care about what they are talking about.* In fact, you have got to *really* care, or else your kids will see right through your act.

For the best results, this listening to your kids has to start when your kids are young. You want to set up a pattern of being open and available to your kids at an early age. This way, when your child gets older and something significant comes up, they have a history of good communication with you. You want them to be comfortable talking about difficult topics with you. If you get upset over the smallest thing, they certainly aren't going to want to talk to you about sensitive issues.

Let me provide an example my sister Mary recently related to me. In her senior year of high school in 1970, Mary got pregnant. This was not the most common thing in those days—and it certainly wasn't talked about much back then, either. Mary told me that Dad started to talk to her and give her advice about the pregnancy. When she reached this part of her story, Mary got really energized, even agitated. Basically, she told me, she was not about to start listening to Dad after he had not bothered to talk to her for years. I was taken aback that Mary had so much passion after over thirty years.

But the lesson here, dads, is to talk to your kids from the time they are little. And talk to them about real stuff. Get into practice talking to them as youngsters. Make it safe for them to come to you and confess or tell you they are struggling. My experience is that so many teens do not confide in their parents because the teens assume (many times rightly so) that their parents will freak out about anything that is outside of what the parents want to believe about them.

There are a couple of basic human behaviors that get in the way of communication. One is that, frankly, most of us don't really listen. We have a little something that gets in the way of actually listening: our brains! We don't seem to know how to turn them off so that we can listen to someone. When someone is talking to us, so often we just wait for them to shut up or take a breath so that we can make our point. Or we may actually let the other person talk, but all the while, we are formulating our response. Or we may just be ignoring them, or thinking about something that happened in the past, or worrying about what we are going to do in the future. We may look at the person talking to us, but our wonderful active brain is busy with other tasks. The brain wants to keep busy, and the other person may be talking so slow, or be so boring, that the brain shifts to other, more "important" stuff.

Another thing that gets in the way of listening is our need to be right. It's as if we are dipped into a vat of self-righteousness when we are born. We want to be right, sometimes at all costs. So when someone talks to us, we often drift into this right/wrong mindset. In our minds, we are not really listening to the other person, but categorizing everything they say into our little right/wrong file: "Well, he's right about that one, but on this other matter he is so wrong" or "Why would she do that when I know a much better way to get that done?" It's sure hard to listen to someone when we are constantly making these silent judgments to ourselves.

"The first liar doesn't have a chance." This is an expression I picked up that is an indication people aren't listening to each other. When one person talks about his vacation, his sick kids, his obnoxious boss, his commute to work, his fishing or hunting trip—anything at all—the next person will talk about how much better or worse her own experience was. These conversations are not about listening—they are about outdoing each other. Start listening to and noticing your own conversations or others'. It will be amazing. And what does it feel like when you tell a story, wanting to do a little bragging or complaining, and the other person just launches into her own story? You don't feel listened to, that's for sure.

Dads want to fix things. This concept came to my attention when I read *Men are from Mars, Women are from Venus.* Now I was surely practicing this concept for a long time, but I wasn't aware of it until I read about it. Men want to provide solutions—it's a way of feeling wanted, needed, useful, and, frankly, masculine. If you come to a man with an apparent problem, he goes into fix-it mode.

Once at dinner, my wife shared with me about an issue she was having at work. She was frustrated that someone in her office had not completed a project to her satisfaction. As Sherry explained the situation to me, I could easily see a "flaw" in her directions and follow-up. So what did I do? I told her what she did wrong. My intent was to "educate" my wife. What actually happened was I made Sherry hopping mad. My way of being with her was about right/wrong and fix-it, rather than about putting myself in her place. She told me later that all she wanted was for me to listen and be empathetic.

So when your children come to you and want to talk, ask them what they want from you. Do they want you to fix the situation? Do they want a solution? Do they just want to vent—you know, just rant and rave to get it out of their system? Do they want a little sympathy? Do they want you to agree with them, no matter what? Find out what they really want and then, just do it!

"Seek first to understand, then to be understood." The "seek first to understand" concept is in all of the Stephen Covey *Seven Habits* books (235). That's how important listening is. The essence of this concept is that if you want someone to understand you, you must first actually listen and understand that person. Once a person feels heard, you earn his trust. Then he will return the favor and really listen to you. Again, we are often so interested in making our case that we don't really listen to what the other person is saying. We usually are waiting for him to stop, or at least hesitate enough so we can interrupt. It seems we are just trying to be right and have no idea what the other person thinks or feels.

In my coaching training, I learned a technique called reflective listening that assists with seeking to understand. Let's say dad and daughter want to discuss a problem or disagreement—a small problem or disagreement, not something huge. Daughter is given two minutes to address a topic. Dad will just listen for the full two minutes. When the daughter is done, the dad then tells her what he heard. If she feels Dad understands, that he actually *gets* it, then the roles are reversed. However, if the daughter doesn't feel Dad understands or gets it, then she offers further explanation or clarification. This process continues until the daughter believes that Dad really, truly expresses what she is saying.

Here's how Darby Saxbe described this technique of reflective listening in *The Oprah Magazine*. (Okay, I confess, I occasionally read Sherry's *O Magazine*.)

> The Most Useful Communication Technique of All Time is deceptively simple, but it works like magic. Next time your partner makes a point, take a moment to digest whatever he is saying. Then say it back to him. Maybe not word for word, but you have to get the gist—and you can't stop trying until your partner agrees you've nailed it. Switch roles and repeat. Once you're not so busy explaining yourself to someone who just doesn't get it, you can look for compromise.
>
> Before I started grad school and officially drank the psychotherapy Kool-Aid, I used to mock this technique as a way to wrap gauze around discord: "I'm hearing that you are a pathetic jerk." "Well, I'm hearing that you are a total loser." But once I tried it, I realized "I'm hearing . . ." isn't just psychobabble. It telegraphs the message, "I'm listening to you, because what you have to tell me is important." (151)

One of the other very basic techniques in listening is to look like you are paying attention. This is my big one. I will be working on the computer, or checking emails, or watching TV—whatever, just something else. Sherry will say something to me, and I will just keep up with whatever I was doing, never even acknowledging her. She doesn't usually believe this when I say it, but I *do* hear her—I just don't give her any evidence that I have heard her. So put down your iPod and your cell phone. Turn off the TV, step away from the computer, put down the paper or magazine. Turn around and actually face your child.

I recommend a couple of books about communication. As I mentioned earlier, any of Stephen Covey's *Seven Habits* books are great resources. I also recommend *Men are from Mars, Women are from Venus* by John Gray and *The Five Love Languages* by Gary Chapman. Chapman says that there are five love languages: acts of service, physical touch, words of affirmation, receiving gifts, and quality time. Gary Chapman goes on to say that we usually show our love and appreciation in the language we like to receive love and appreciation. When we do this, the other person may not speak our language. For instance, my language is physical touch, while Sherry's is acts of service. Sherry does so much for me, and I want a little physical contact. I try to hug her, and all she wants me to do is to take out the garbage and recycling.

The Bradshaw model

Here is a very simple and effective conflict resolution tool that we introduce to the teens and parents in the parent-child seminars.

The Bradshaw model takes a little time to get used to, but once you have become proficient at it, it can become a way of thinking. It will be natural. There are five simple steps:

I saw or I heard

I interpreted (what did I make up?)

I feel or I felt

I want

I learned

Let me go over each of the steps in more detail.

I saw or I heard. This step is "just the facts, ma'am," and it can be the most difficult for many. Why? Two reasons. First, because we are quick to make judgments and interpretations of what we see and hear. Second, when there's conflict, we generally want to be right, and we do that by making the other person wrong. So in this step, I ask people to just describe the incident or situation as if they were watching it on video; no interpretations or judgments, just "what did you see?" When I walk people through the Bradshaw model, I find myself doing a lot of interrupting in people's descriptions because they unconsciously start interpreting.

"My daughter looked sad," a parent will say.

"No," I say, "just describe her physical characteristics."

"My son looked apprehensive," the parent will venture the next time.

Again, I say, "No . . . what physical characteristic did you observe that lead you to that conclusion?" Then the parent will describe how he or she observed the teen's head hanging down, or how the teen wasn't looking up. No smiling or waving. That's just the facts!

I interpreted. Okay, now's the time to let all your interpretations go wild. What did you make up? What did you assume?

We all see the world through our unique set of glasses or filters. That is, we all interpret things in our own unique way. And yet we think that is how everyone thinks. No! You are the only person in the world with your particular set of experiences and background. But when we think everyone sees the world as we do, we assume that the people we are talking to interpret what we say in the same way we intend to be understood. When we both talk *and* listen, our minds go faster than the spoken words; our minds start to fill in the empty spaces. I don't know about you, but when I talk, I assume everything that is going on in my mind has somehow been communicated to the listener, as if he or she has ESP!

I felt. This is where the real work gets done, where resolution can occur. So often, when we have conflict, we immediately go into the blame game: "Well, you did this," and "Oh, yeah, well, you did this other thing." And then we go spinning out of control and end up talking about some event that occurred long ago.

Resolution can only occur when we talk about the feeling. This is the time to tell the other person how you felt. But be careful, this is *not* about blaming. Expressing your feeling might sound like, "I felt disrespected"; not, "You disrespected me." Remember, no one can *make* you feel anything—you choose to feel disrespected.

One final note about the word "feelings." Feelings tend to be described by one word: "I feel lonely"; "I feel angry"; "I feel depressed"; "I feel ignored." I often hear people say things like, "I feel like you ignored me" or "I feel like you don't care about me." These two statements are really beliefs. To get to feelings, answer the question, "How does it feel when you were ignored?" or "How does it feel that the other person doesn't care about you?"

I want. Now, here is your chance to ask for what you actually want. Too often, I hear people just wanting to complain and to make the other person wrong. You have to get away from your self-righteousness here and actually ask for what you want. Often, what you want is imbedded in a complaint. If you find yourself complaining, ask yourself, What it is that would make the complaint go away? Sometimes nothing will make complainers happy—they just really want to complain and insist that others are wrong. Just complaining will not resolve anything.

I learned (about myself). Ah, yes, the final and most important step. What is so important about learning about yourself? If you don't want anything to change, or if you want to keep having conflict, argument, and drama, this step isn't important. However, if you do want something to be different, if you want to learn about yourself and grow, then take a look at your patterns. Do you do this same thing often? What are your beliefs about yourself? What assumptions do you make when talking or listening to people?

Let me give you an example from my personal life of how I used the Bradshaw model with someone who wasn't aware of it. When I left my architecture company to go into seminar facilitation, I transferred my old employer's 401(k) to an IRA with a personal investment adviser. The process took around two months, and it took a lot of phone calls and forms on my part. I told my adviser that I wanted the fifty-eight thousand dollars put into something steady and boring—a money market or high-quality bond. No stocks, for sure.

The transfer was made in late February 2007, and by the time I checked in with my financial guy, on February 26, thirty thousand dollars worth of stock had been bought. Well, on February 27, the Dow went down 415.3 points (3.3 percent)—the entire stock market took a huge dive.

When I found this out, I was beside myself. I was livid. I wanted to lash out at just about anyone. I was mad at my adviser for not communicating my desires to anyone else in his office. I was mad that he had left his twenty-eight-year-old son to handle my hard-earned money. I was kicking myself big time. I have never liked putting my money in the stock market; it brought back memories of the stock market crash of October 1987. I was literally ill after that 25 percent drop in the markets. I was regretting that I had even left my well-paying, steady, reliable job as an engineer. I ranted to Sherry that I was going to withdraw all of our savings and find someplace else to put it. This sure qualified as having conflict, at least on my part.

But notice that a lot of my interpretations and emotions were not even about the event. They were about things that had gone on in my past.

Once Sherry calmed me down, I called my financial guy. Actually, I talked to his son because his dad was on vacation. I decided I would go through the Bradshaw model with the son, but not explain it—just go through it on my side. I first told him the facts: what I had requested concerning where I wanted my savings invested, and how his office had always checked in with me in the past before any large transactions were initiated (the "I heard, I saw" step).

I then talked about my interpretations. I told the son that I assumed they would check with me like they had always done. I told him I assumed that once I spoke with one person in the office, everyone in the office would know my wishes. I assumed that his dad would always be handling my account, not his son.

Then I told the son how I felt. The only thing I said was, "I don't feel taken care of." The impact this simple statement had was amazing. The son stopped giving me excuses and stories. He got quiet. He said simply, "We will make it right." He didn't say exactly how, but I could tell from the tone in his voice that something had shifted in him.

Then I said that I wanted my original intentions to be

honored. That is, I wanted all of the money to go to a money market or bond fund. After I got off the phone, I couldn't imagine how I could actually get what I wanted. Someone would have to lose money, and I figured the only person it could be was me.

A few days later, my regular financial advisor was back in town and gave me a call. He said that his company would sell all the stock and put everything in money market or bonds, as requested, and that they—not me—would take any loss incurred. I got exactly what I asked for.

This incident was a serious learning experience. I realized that I had never put my requests on this transfer of my retirement savings into writing, not even e-mail. I only told one person. I also never asked what would happen or where my transferred money would go. Basically, I didn't treat my own money as if it was all that important to me.

In explaining the situation to me, my financial advisor, the dad, shared all the assumptions made on his side and what his company had learned from the situation. The dad had gone through most of the Bradshaw model seemingly without realizing it.

One last word of caution: when you start using these listening techniques, don't be stiff and formal. If you pull your son or daughter to the side and say, "Let's have some open communication," it won't work. Just start practicing the techniques. Others will notice, and they will ask you about what you're doing.

–12–

Dads and Sports

THIS COULD VERY well be the "Dads and Fishing" chapter, or the "Dads and Hunting" chapter, or the "Dads and Music" chapter. Actually, it is really the "Do Some Activity with Your Kid" chapter. But, since I love sports so much, I am going to talk about dads and sports. Sports can be a great activity for bonding, a fantastic learning experience, and a way to build self-esteem. You will see in the following stories that sports created lifelong connections between dads and children.

In reading a couple of the *Chicken Soup* books, I found many examples of dads making lifelong connections with their sons and daughters. In *Chicken Soup for the Soul, The Wisdom of Fathers*, there are numerous stories of how fishing created lifelong connections between Dad and kids. In one touching story a daughter makes her final hospital visit to see here dying dad. As he laid there, seemingly asleep or unconscious, she began to hum a song. This was the song Dad had sung to her—loudly to wake her when she was a kid. After she finished singing, her dad didn't budge. But then he opened his eyes, he spoke about the song, and closed his eyes again. Dad died five hours later, but by singing to his daughter as a child, he had created this special moment for her at the end of his life. (Canfield & Hansen)

Again, this connection can be made through things other than sports. The key is to create connections.

As I was putting this chapter together, I was surprised at the cascade effect of my dad's introducing me to a sport. But the concepts and lessons presented here can be applied to dads, kids, and any activities. When dads participate with their kids in sports or other activities, relationships can be enhanced, lessons taught, and lifelong bonds created.

I went to my first major league baseball game and my first NFL game with my dad—just him and me. None of the other kids in the family went. The realization of this memory is in direct conflict with what I have believed for so long: that I was not "special," not my dad's favorite, after my two brothers and three sisters were born.

Sometime between 1957 and 1959, my dad took me to Tiger Stadium in Detroit for a Sunday doubleheader between the Tigers and the New York Yankees. We had seats directly behind home plate. When I think about it, those seats may have been the best seats I ever had at a major league baseball game. It's funny the few things I actually remember about the game. I can remember being behind the plate and seeing the foul ball screen. The only other vivid memory I have is of going to the bathroom with my dad between games. It was a mob scene. (Imagine a wide-eyed seven-year-old going to a public restroom for the first time.) Then my dad did something that now bugs me as an adult—he made some clever remark, out loud, to no one in particular, about so many guys having to pee all at the same time. It's the kind of remark that I would make now.

As I have said earlier, as dads, we never know when the lessons we teach our kids will show up in their lives. One thing that showed up for me right away was my love for baseball. I played baseball from the time I was eight or nine until I got to high school. I am a big baseball fan to this day. When Mickey Mantle was having liver problems and eventually died in 1995, I was stunned that I had a memory of the New York Yankees' starting lineup: Mantle, Yogi Berra, Bobby Richardson, Moose Skowron, and Whitey Ford. Yet all my life, I never admitted I liked the Yankees. In fact, I was one of the many non-New Yorker Yankee-haters. But because of that early experience in Tiger Stadium, I knew all the Yankees of that era.

Late in 1959, when we moved to the Maryland suburbs outside of Washington DC, my love of baseball continued. I remember going to a game in DC at old Griffith Stadium. Given that it was Griffith Stadium, the players were the original Senators, not the expansion team that came in 1961. Here is another weird thing about memories: the only thing I remember about that game is walking into the game, down this alley with high brick walls and buildings on each side. I remember another kid say something about Mickey Mantle's long home run. When I Googled "Mantle Griffith Stadium blast," I found a Web site that listed Mantle's ten longest home runs. The Griffith Stadium home run occurred on April 15, 1953, and measured 565 feet. The Web site said that this was the home run that coined the phrase "tape measure homerun."

Just after our family moved to Maryland, the Senators moved to Minnesota to become the Twins, but there was still an expansion team in the DC area. As a ten-year-old, none of this made sense. As I got a little older, we started going to Senator games at DC Stadium. I joined a group called the

Knot-Hole Club, which was sponsored by the *Washington Star*, an afternoon newspaper I delivered for six years. There were about six or seven Saturday games a year, and we could go for about $1.50. Now, here's a memory that's not too pleasant. My younger brother Richard and I, along with a couple of friends, went to a game. We brought a baseball along with us to get autographs after the game. I remember Jimmy Pearsall telling me to "get the heck away from him."

As we were milling around looking for players, we started to brag about the ball being a foul ball we had caught. Real smart! A bunch of kids decided they wanted to take the ball from us. So we ran, even throwing the ball between us to keep away from these kids, but eventually they caught us and took the ball. I recall buying the darn thing back from them. But the real fun happened when we missed our ride home and we decided to walk home, all six miles. At the time it felt like it was twenty miles away. We eventually walked over three miles in the wrong direction. We were lost, the police were looking for us, and we eventually found a pay phone and got picked up just before dark. Still, quite a story to tell after all this time.

I also passed this ritual of going to major league baseball games on to my kids. When we moved back to Maryland in 1985, we went to a number of Baltimore Orioles games at old Memorial Stadium.

While living in Columbia, Maryland, Sherry, Keith, and Jesse attended a fundraiser basketball game featuring some of the Oriole players, including Cal Ripken. Keith got his picture in the local newspaper; the shot shows him poring over his baseball cards with a neighbor kid. One year, my company's summer picnic was at a water park. One of the attractions was Billy Ripken, Cal's brother, who played second base for the Orioles at the time. We took Jesse and had him sit on poor Billy's lap for a picture. I say "poor Billy" because Jesse had a wet swimsuit on and Billy complained pretty loudly.

Our Billy-Ripken connection continued back to the Northwest. We went to a game in the Kingdome in Seattle and went looking for autographs of Orioles players after the game. Keith and I found Billy, but he was surrounded by a bunch of teens. Keith, who was around ten at the time and short for his age, couldn't get Billy's attention. I was off to the side, watching the teens put their cards in Billy's face. Keith was at an entirely different level, much lower, with this adoring and expectant look on his face. Billy kept taking the bigger kids' baseballs or cards, but Keith hung in there. Finally, I said to Billy, "How about the little kid?"

Billy looked at me and said, "Are you his agent?"

I thought about a lot of different things to say, but I just came back with, "No, I'm just his dad." Billy obliged, and Keith now has a Billy Ripken autograph somewhere.

How about 1988? The Orioles lost something like eighteen or twenty-one games in a row to start the season. They were just awful. So the team decided to stage a Fan Appreciation Night. We got seats in the upper deck along the right field foul line. In the middle of the game, Cal Ripken comes to the plate when, suddenly, the crowd starts to go wild. We looked down below us, and there jogging—or maybe it was prancing—in from right field was Morganna, the Kissing Bandit. How did we know it was Morganna? Well, she's very recognizable; that is all I need to say. She really took her time making her way to home plate. The crowd went absolutely nuts. I don't recall who the Orioles played or who won, but I remember Morganna kissing Cal Ripkin.

Sometime in the early '90s, we went to a family reunion in Southern Wisconsin—Lake Geneva, I believe. We decided to make a big vacation out of it and include a baseball game in Chicago. I wanted to buy tickets from someone off the street around the park, which I find exciting. The first guy wanted too much, so we kept going. Suddenly, I realized it was a very well attended game. It was a turn-back-the-clock game: old uniforms and all the other things that were postponed from the year before because of a strike. I went back, found the guy, and bought four tickets—upper deck along the right field line. The White Sox were playing the hated Yankees. Early in the game, the Sox loaded the bases, and up came John Kruk. This guy was seriously out of shape. We could tell from the cheap seats that it was him in an old-timer's uniform. He even said he was out of shape. John said this great line to a heckler during spring training. This woman said something about his lack of fitness or conditioning for being a professional athlete. He shot back: "I'm not an athlete, I'm a baseball player." Anyway, Kruk hit this towering home run—a grand slam—and, of course, the place just went wild.

We took a number of trips to Seattle for Mariners games. For a while, it was an annual thing. Once, when I made hotel arrangements as we drove up to Seattle, I thought I had just settled for any old place because I had made reservations so late. It was the Crown Plaza. When we checked in, we saw all these people standing outside on the sidewalk, kind of milling around. Turns out, the Crown Plaza hotel is where all the visiting teams stay when they play in Seattle. We had access to the hotel lobby since we were guests, but the autograph-seekers had to stay outside. It was great for me, as an adult, to see the players hanging out. My kids were beside themselves. For the next few years, we made a point of staying at the same hotel when we went to a Mariners game. Once when the Orioles were in town, I was hoping to see Ray Miller, the pitching coach. I had once heard he had gone to the same high school I had attended.

I always do like the local connection. Harold Reynolds grew up in Corvallis and played for many years with the Seattle Mariners. I also knew Harold's younger brother, Tim. We played a little slow-pitch softball together, and we both refereed high school football. Harold signed with the Orioles in the mid-1980s. When we went to one of their games, we sought out Harold. He had a crowd around him when I mentioned Corvallis, Oregon. He stopped in his tracks and turned toward us. I told Harold I had played a little softball with his brother Tim. (I left out the part about how bad I was.) Since we had nothing for him to autograph, or anything for him to write with, Harold helped us get a pen and some paper, and he gave us an autograph.

Just notice all of these baseball and sports connections I have with my kids because of that game my dad took me to in Detroit in 1957. Whenever I talk to my sons, we always seem to talk about the latest sports news. Again, it's a great connection.

The first NFL game I went to was at DC Stadium when the Redskins were pretty bad—in the early '60s, pre-Sonny Jurgensen. The funny thing about this game is that I don't remember who the Redskins played, or where we sat. All I can remember is Santa parachuting into the game at halftime.

Weird, the things we remember. This experience wasn't the beginning of my love of football; it just reinforced my enthusiasm for the game. I played eighty-five-pound football as an eleven-year-old and won a trophy for most valuable lineman. I was sick for the awards ceremony, so my coaches came over to my house. Seeing them walk through the front door was amazing.

I played youth football until I got to high school and played two years on varsity—on a lousy team—but I still loved it. I liked football so much that I refereed youth, high school, and college football for over thirty years. Watching the Redskins became more than just a thing to do on Sunday; it was a ritual. I can remember how upset we got when, in 1978, one of the games was preempted by the coverage of the funeral of Pope Paul VI. Later, I took watching the Skins a bit too far when I damaged a relationship with a friend by asking, "Don't you check the sports page before calling?"

Nonetheless, football and sports in general have become a connection between me and my sons. But it didn't just start with my family. My brother Pat is nearly ten years younger than me. When I was in my early twenties, I took Pat to a number of sporting events. We went to a new, big, indoor track meet at the University of Maryland. I remember seeing Kip Keino, winner of the 1968 Olympic 1500-meter race. We also went to an NCAA Lacrosse Championship at Johns Hopkins University when the University of Maryland played Navy. In 1974, I talked Pat into coming along with me from Maryland to see the final round of the U.S. Open at Winged Foot Golf in Westchester, New York. I was a big Arnold Palmer fan, and he was close to the lead. Unfortunately, Arnie faded down the stretch, but so did a lot of big names.

I specifically remember Gary Player three-putting the ninth hole and taking himself out of contention.

Bottom line is, my dad exposed me to a number of sports, and I didn't just take an interest in athletics for myself as a player and spectator—I also shared this love of sports with my brother, my sons, and my wife, although Sherry was already a pretty big sports fan when I met her. Since we had something in common, Sherry and I could do things together.

Fishing. I can only remember going fishing twice as a kid: once with my dad in Southern Maryland and once with my uncle Roger in Northern Virginia. For some reason, I got the idea that, as a dad, it was my duty to take my kids fishing. So, without a lot of knowledge of fishing, I took my son Keith fishing in a little lake (or maybe it was more of a pond) in Columbia, Maryland. This was not a serious fishing lake. It was a man-made lake in a common area between housing developments, and there was a nice walking path around the shore.

I did not have any bait, so I got some frozen corn from the freezer and off we went. Keith was about seven or eight at the time, so I handled much of the baiting and casting duties. At some point, we got a bite. I don't remember much about reeling the fish in. I do have a vivid memory of struggling to get the hook out of the fish's mouth. As I struggled, feeling totally incompetent, a group of people came by. A woman who knew what she was doing freed the hook—or rather, the fish—in seconds. My embarrassment of not being able to get a hook out of a fish's mouth didn't last long, because she simply took the little three- or four-inch sunfish and tossed it back into the lake. I mean, what were we going to do with that little fish anyway? But as the fish hit the water, Keith looked around in shock and said, "My fish!" The hurt on his face just stopped this helpful woman and me. The woman and I looked at each other in amazement and embarrassment. Keith was crushed. Later, we were able to laugh about it, but in that moment, Keith looked like he had lost his prized possession. But now, Keith and I have a lasting memory because of my feeble effort to make sure I did the required dad-duty of fishing with my son.

When I mentioned fishing to my younger brother, Pat, he remembered going crabbing. Now, that was fun! I remembered how we kids would tie a string to a chicken neck and throw it into the water. Once we knew we had a crab on the chicken neck, we would slowly bring in the line. Then an adult, usually Dad, would slowly dip the net into the water behind the crab and scoop it up.

Now Jeanne, Pat's wife, had quite a different experience fishing with her dad. She lived in Alaska and her dad would take the family fishing every weekend. She described her family of five sitting in a boat made for four adults. She was the youngest, so they had her just sitting in the bottom of the boat. She said it was cold and she had to pee in a coffee can while the guys just took care of business over the side of the boat. Fishing for her was a gasoline-smelling, cold, unpleasant experience.

Pat talked to a guy who went hunting a lot with his dad as a kid. Yet as an adult, he didn't go hunting. He said he went hunting to spend time with his dad, not necessarily to go hunting. As I have been saying, it's not necessarily the activity—it's the interaction. But, as Jeanne experienced, it's got to be something the kids might actually enjoy.

Golf. I don't know if my dad initiated it, but I got involved in golf as a teen. I got a set of new clubs and took lessons at the golf course at the Andrews Air Force Base. I remember my dad dropping me off at my first golf outing at Andrews and picking me up afterward. I recall him talking to the threesome I joined, or maybe he talked to the starter. My dad also set me up with our neighbor, Mr. Zepp, who took me golfing quite a few times.

In high school, I played golf with a bunch of buddies. I continued to play in college at the University of Maryland course. After college, I played with friends quite often.

The point is, none of this would have happened if it hadn't been for my dad introducing me to golf when I was a teen.

The dreaded "sports dad"

Now as much as I like sports, a balance is really required. Who hasn't heard of a dad who took their child's sports "career" too far? Here's a definition of a sports dad.

> **Sports dad:** commonly-seen dad who is obsessed with his child's athletic ability. These dads can become highly aggressive when their children do something wrong in a sport, such as "pitching the ball an inch too far to the right." These dads are obviously living their lives through their sons and daughters, just because *they* didn't make it to the pros.
>
> From: http://www.urbandictionary.com (Sollabec)

The only thing I would add to the above definition is that the obsessed sports dad wants to live vicariously through his child.

You must have seen or heard a story of a sports dad going out of control. A recent incident was captured on video and, of course, put on the Internet: a coach, a dad of one of his players, comes onto the football field, hits, and knocks down a youngster from the opposing team. Now this is an extreme example, but the obsessed dad is out there.

I refereed football for over thirty years, from intramurals while I was in college to youth football to high school, and, finally, Division II and III college games. I sure saw my share of these crazed dads. The crazy thing about the football dads was that they often made refereeing the youth football games more of a pain than officiating high school games. It broke down that way because in the youth games, parents can stand right on the sidelines. In high school and college, most of the fans are sitting in the stands or are standing a significant distance from the field. My fellow referees used to say that working the youth games would be okay if we could just keep the parents from attending.

After all the games I have done, one incident sticks out in my mind. I was a volunteer soccer referee for my kids' American Youth Soccer Organization (AYSO) league. The entire idea of AYSO soccer is to just teach kids about sports and soccer; the competition aspect is played down. In my town of Corvallis, Oregon, the newspaper stopped publishing the league's results and standings to downplay the competition. Everything about AYSO is on a volunteer basis. Every parent is expected to volunteer for some activity, from coaching to refereeing to bringing halftime refreshments. As I left a game and headed to my car, a coach I knew ran after to me to complain about a call. Yet this guy's team had won the game!

Again, I think the key here is the balance—encouraging the kids and pushing them without being nuts. Sports dads could take a lesson from Archie Manning.

In Archie and Payton Manning's book *Manning*, which was written before either Peyton or Eli won a Super Bowl,

Archie talks about his arm's-length approach at his kids' games. Now, here's an All-Pro NFL quarterback dad (Archie, that is), and he says he *never* acted out at his kids' games. In fact, Archie stated that he only twice had conversations with his kids' coaches. Archie, a former NFL MVP, had the credentials to say something to coaches and other parents, yet he worked hard at not being the obsessive sports dad. One theme in the book discusses the Manning's priorities in life. Both Archie and Payton stated that their priorities are faith, family, friends, and then (and only then), sports and football—in that order! Football comes fourth.

Another thing I found interesting was Archie's attitude about youth sports. First, he said, first and foremost, youth sports should be *fun*—fun for the kids, that is. How often do dads forget that? The other amazing thing is that Archie insisted the boys not participate in organized sports until around the seventh or eighth grade. He never pressured his sons to participate in any sports. When they did participate, Archie did insist that they complete what they started. Archie was also available for his three sons if they wanted advice or guidance. Now, imagine it: Archie Manning has this fairly laid-back attitude, no pressure on the kids, and he has two Super Bowl MVP sons. All of the obsessive dads could take quite a lesson here.

In his book *Buried Lies*, Peter Jacobsen expresses a similar approach to youth sports. Peter says parents often ask him at what age their budding golfer offspring should be winning tournaments. Peter responds by advising parents not to put timetables on their kids, to let them have a little fun instead. They're kids, for goodness's sake.

What is it that makes a dad get so obsessive about his kids and sports? An easy answer is that dad wants to live his sports life vicariously through his kids. Perhaps dad feels his self-worth is dependent upon his children's athletic abilities. Maybe it's our culture.

In the few short months between December 2007 and February 2008, I read three stories of sports obsession: a dad was arrested for restraining his son for an hour with tape and taping a Packers Jersey onto him (Cops: Dad Arrested for Taping Packers Jersey to Son, 7); three people were killed after an argument following the 2008 Super Bowl (3rd Man Dies In Shooting At Largo Retail Center); a high school senior in Nevada made up a lie that he had been recruited by the Cal and Oregon football programs—even staged a fake news conference to announce his decision (Nevada high school football recruit made up story).

Then there are the numerous stories of a dad storming onto the field at his kid's game—be it baseball, football, or hockey—to attack a referee, a coach, or a kid.

Thankfully, there are dads out there who keep sports in perspective. I am all for sports, number one, just for the physical fitness benefits. Plus, there are some great life lessons to be learned, such as how to build character, how to stay determined not to give up, and how to work as part of a team. But sports being the most important thing in life is, I believe, a sign of misplaced priorities. Most sports careers end by the time the athlete is forty, and frankly, there are not many athletes that make it that long. I think back to my years refereeing football, when I saw how few kids moved from high school sports to play for a small college. The number of young athletes who go on to Division I college is even smaller. The percentage of players who go from college to the pros is also small. Then there are the debilitating injuries. The injuries can happen in an instant.

Once a player's career is over, then what? If everything has been put on a sports career, it's a shock to have to work for a living. I have included a couple of stories of dads who encouraged their kids to participate in sports, but you will notice that these dads didn't push their children and kept sports in perspective.

Archie Manning

I picked up his book *Manning* to see what kind of sports dad Archie Manning was. I was surprised to read on the first page that his dad committed suicide when Archie was a sophomore at Old Miss. The message I got from reading the book was that this incident caused Archie to put things into perspective. Yes, Archie liked sports and saw the benefits they offered, but he also saw that family was more important. This importance of family over sports hit home again when his oldest son Cooper's career at the University of Mississippi was cut short because of a spinal condition.

Now listen up, Dads. Archie was an All-Pro NFL quarterback. He probably had a lot to offer his kids' coaches, but he gave both his kids and their coaches the freedom to do their thing without his interference. Peyton went on to win the 2007 Super Bowl, and Eli won the 2008 Super Bowl. You don't have to be a crazed dad to have your children make it to the top levels of professional sports.

Peter Jacobsen

Peter has been a PGA professional golfer for over twenty years. In *Buried Lies*, he talks about how his dad, Erling, introduced him to golf. Erling made golf available to Peter, but he didn't insist that his son play. The Jacobsen family took their golf very seriously, but, as Erling told Peter near the end of his life, "The most important part of golf is a sense of humor."(6)

Devan and Dave Doan

When I first got a high definition TV I couldn't get enough. One day I saw an ESPN program entitled, *Timeless*. It told several compelling stories of young athletes. I was struck by the story of Devan Doan, a high school girl competing in the World Bench Press Championships in Cleveland. I was curious as to how her dad had influenced her interest in weight lifting. The following is my telephone interview with Devan and Dave Doan.

> **Dave:** *I got involved in weightlifting just through sports in high school, but I didn't know anything about competitive lifting until well after college. I was at the YMCA, and a couple of guys asked if I was going to be in the bench press competition. I didn't even know what that was, so I just brushed them off. Every week, they kept asking me about it. So finally I said, "Okay, I'll do it. I'll try it, just tell me what I've got to do." I actually did pretty well at it. So I got my start in competitive lifting by not knowing anything.*
>
> *From there it just grew. I started to go to local meets. I think my third meet was the U.S. Nationals, and I took third place in that. I thought, This is pretty easy. So I kept on doing it. By then, Devan was coming to every meet, and we made it a family thing. At nationals every year, we would drive and go camping for a week and make a vacation out of it.*
>
> *In the twenty years I have been competing, Devan has only missed a handful of events. When Devan was about twelve, she started to take an interest in*

weightlifting. She's the one who instigated it. It was in-
teresting, because I had never thought about training a
girl. The equipment fits differently. So I thought I would
learn right along with her.

Devan: *I grew up watching my dad lift. I think every*
girl growing up wants to go to the Olympics and win a
gold medal. A lot of girls like gymnastics or ice-skating,
things like that. I found out that I had no talent whatso-
ever to do anything like that. But I wanted to go to the
Olympics. Then I realized, with power lifting, I could win
tournaments and go to things like the Olympics and be
like my dad. My dad was very supportive, but he made it
clear that I didn't have to do this because he was doing
it. He said he wanted me to do it because I wanted to do
it. He was very encouraging. He even said he wouldn't
be mad or disappointed if I decided to stop. He certainly
pushed me to do better, because he knew I had potential.
He pushed me to succeed because he knew I wanted to
succeed. He was pushing me for me, not for him. He defi-
nitely was not trying to live his life through me. I might
have been trying to be like my dad sometimes.

Dave: *Her first real meet was as a freshman in high*
school. She did the squat, dead lift, and bench for high
school. Wisconsin, by the way, has the largest high
school power-lifting program in the country. Her school
didn't have a lifting program. In fact, her school didn't
even encourage her lifting. So much so that the athletic
director didn't let her use the weight room at the school
because she wasn't involved in school sports.

Devan: *But in my senior year, I took a weightlifting class*
taught by the athletic director, just for a little get-back.

Dave: *In her first meet, she did very well. She got first* place. In her sophomore year, she won the U.S. Nationals—varsity! That sophomore year was the first year she made the U.S. Adult Bench Press championship team. She has made that team every year since.

Every time we traveled, I made sure we went someplace historical, so she could learn something. We still do that. The world championships are typically in Europe. We've been to Europe eight times. She's been everywhere from Paris to Auschwitz, even Communist countries. She's had a lot of opportunities from what she's done.

It made me feel good to see her doing so well. It's an accomplishment—for her. It's always good to see your kid do well at things. It was a great feeling of success for me, but it's also a great feeling for her that she got some success, and she can build on that in everything she does in her life.

In lifting, a young girl has to get up in front of everyone and tell how much she weighs. That's a difficult thing for a young girl to do. At the competition, they weigh everybody and put it up on the big screen and tell everybody. That was an interesting hurdle for Devan to get over.

She got picked on quite a lot in high school for lifting. It bothered her somewhat. But by then, she was having a lot of success in it. She was getting to do a lot of things and see a lot of things that these other kids would never see or do. It irritated her a bit, but didn't bother her at the end. It's one of those things—when you're successful, you don't have to say anything. They all knew Devan had done something special.

Devan: *I did break my hip in high school from lifting. So* *now I concentrate on the bench press, which has always been my forte—and my dad's. I am going to school at the University of Wisconsin Oshkosh, going for nursing. I work as a nurse's aide at a hospital, and I am coaching a girls lifting team at my high school's rival. When my dad coached me, there were often things he said that I didn't like. Sometimes I catch myself saying the exact same things to my girls and I think, Oh, my god, I sound just like my dad. I am going to the world championships in Luxemburg in May 2009—my eighth world's. It's back to where my first championship was. [She took the silver medal.]*

The teasing in high school did affect me for a while. I think all girls have self-esteem problems, and when someone picks on you, it's a blow. But it also fired me up to be more driven to succeed, because I knew I had something those kids didn't have. I had the opportunities to do things those kids never had. I also had a relationship with my dad that most girls don't have. I had a coach, a dad, and a bond that no one else had. I think all this teasing drove me to do better, because I wanted to show myself that this is what I truly loved. It didn't matter what anyone thought, because I loved what it did for me and my family.

The Refereeing Santis

I met Aaron while we were both members of the Northwest Intercollegiate Football Officials Association (NIFOA). Aaron was attending graduate school at the University of Oregon at the time. Aaron was by far the youngest member of the association. What struck me was just how mature and cool under pressure he was. Later I met his dad John, also a member of the NIFOA and figured dad had some influence on Aaron's football refeering. Here are my interviews with Aaron and John.

Part one: Aaron Santi. Aaron started refereeing high school football three months after he graduated from high school. He started refereeing small college football when he was twenty. At the age of twenty-eight, Aaron began working PAC-10 football games. Just after his thirty-fourth birthday, Aaron worked his fifth bowl game, the Cotton Bowl in Dallas in January 2009. He has also worked the Sugar Bowl in January 2006, the Alamo Bowl in December 2006, and the Chick-fil-A Bowl in December 2007. Not bad!

How did Aaron get to the highest levels of college football refereeing at such an early age?

> *It was really through my dad. I started as a Little League umpire when I was in high school. My dad encouraged me to umpire as a way to make a little extra money.*
>
> *As I progressed in high school, I moved up and started umpiring Babe Ruth leagues. I played baseball, basketball, and football in high school. After I graduated, I wanted to stay involved, so Dad suggested I come out and referee high school football. A couple of years later, I started working junior college games in Northern California.*
>
> *Once I started working college games, I worked three or four games a year with my dad. I felt just a little more pressure than I did in games where he wasn't there. I knew, after the game, Dad would give me feedback. I am sure Dad was a little concerned about me, but when the game gets going, we all have our own jobs to do. But*

here I was, in my twenties, working with guys in their forties and fifties. I felt I had to prove myself to a lot of the other referees.

I never got any pressure from Dad to referee. In fact, when I came home with a flyer about umpiring Little League back in high school, Dad didn't push me to do it. But he did help me improve, and got me connected once I got involved. I think the only pressure on me was self-imposed. Dad did say I should enjoy whatever level of football I am working—otherwise, what's the point?

I never really went to any of the games he refereed until I was in high school. When I was playing JV basketball in high school, my dad would occasionally referee the varsity game. It was definitely a little awkward with my friends when we were all at a varsity game and my dad would make a call against our team.

Now my older son (ten years old) loves to come to my games. He wants to come to all my games. I've taken him to CAL, Oregon, and Oregon State. He even comes to the small college games. He just loves the game of football and likes to be around it. My younger son (six years old) isn't as excited about going to the games. I did take him to an Oregon versus Oregon State game. He liked the atmosphere, but he doesn't really care that much about the game. Neither of them get all that excited to see me on TV; by now, it's old hat for them.

When I'm out there coaching my son's Little League team, it boggles my mind how seriously some parents take it. It's just little kids learning to play baseball and having fun.

I was very fortunate to get into the PAC-10 when I did.

Part two: John Santi. *I never pushed either one of my kids to either play sports or to referee. I didn't believe in that. I just let them do their own thing. I figured growing up was tough enough; they don't need any pressure from Mom or Dad to go in one direction or another.*

Once Aaron decided to get into officiating, it became—in my mind—my job to help him out. I wanted to expose him to everything I could. I was very fortunate to be exposed to some pretty good individuals in the officiating business. That's one of the first things I made sure of, was that Aaron got to know them and was exposed to the same people.

My younger son, Dan, two and half years younger than Aaron, is a high school football referee. He'd like to do the small college football, but the demands of his family with two young kids hasn't allowed that yet.

I was always very proud of Aaron. The opportunity to work with Aaron was very satisfying. But once the game got started, I didn't look at Aaron any different than any of the other officials on the field. I really didn't look over my shoulder to see if he was all right. I had enough to worry about, covering my own position. I couldn't be worrying about Aaron—or anyone else, for that matter.

It was always a lifelong dream for me to work in the PAC-10, but that didn't work out. But when Aaron got the word, I was so excited for him. It was one of the proudest moments for me. But you know, I have always been nothing but proud of my two sons.

I had both of my kids pretty young, and I got a later start in refereeing, so family didn't get in the way. My wife Marsha was pretty understanding. It really takes an understanding spouse to be a referee.

> *As much as we think sports, they are important, it's*
> *really a pretty small part of one's life.*

How did John get exposed to officiating? His father-in-law, a high school football referee!

Lessons:

1. Let your kids have fun playing sports.
2. Don't criticize; heck, maybe don't even talk about their games. If they want advice, you know what? They will come to you.
3. Support, encourage, and guide your sons and daughters, but don't ram anything down their throats. Let them decide what sports they really want to do. It's their lives, *not* yours. My parents exposed me to a lot of activities and sports.
   - Baseball
   - Football
   - Square dancing (yuck!)
   - Cub Scouts: I mostly liked this, except for the time I had to dress up in an Indian chief's outfit. Jesse was in the Scouts, but Keith didn't want to participate.
   - Golf: boy, I loved the fact that I could play golf as a kid. Now, I sometimes regret I didn't take it farther.
   - Piano: Maybe it was too soon for me to play at eight. That might be something fun to do now.
   - Trumpet: I was a pretty good trumpet player. I didn't appreciate what my parents did for me there. My dad didn't make a lot of money, and there were six of us kids, but they bought me a trumpet and paid for lessons, some private, for a number of years.
   - Catholic altar boy: what can I say?
   - Music: besides providing me lessons in piano and trumpet, my parents took us to concerts in Washington, DC.

The ones I remember the most are the ones on Sunday evenings, at what we called Watergate concerts. This was in the '60s, well before the Nixon Administration Watergate break-ins. We would sit on a set of big steps and watch bands, usually the Navy band that was set up on a floating stage in the Potomac River. I remember seeing Lee's Mansion across the river in Virginia.

- Museums: imagine—I lived just ten miles from the Capitol Building and twelve miles from the Washington Monument. We used to go to downtown DC all the time. I walked up the steps to the top of the Washington Monument. We visited the Capitol when Congress was in session. I'm sure we went to the White House. Then there were the museums—the Smithsonian and the National Art Gallery.

- Historical sites: well, there were sure lots of them where I grew up, and we definitely went to many of them. There were times, however, where I was none too thrilled to go to these. But as much as I hated these visits, at times, it really stuck. Around 2000, I decided I wanted to visit the Custer battlefield in Montana. I realized my family wouldn't be as thrilled as me, so I went alone. It was great. I visited every visitor's center and information sign. I saw a family with a dad as thrilled as me, but he was dragging his bored kids and wife around. I also went to Mount Rushmore when a business trip took me to South Dakota. The things you do with your kids stay with them. It just may be a few years before it shows up.

4. Go to their games/activities.

In the book *Manning*, Archie talked about going to nearly every one of his three kids' games—easy enough to do when the boys were in junior and senior high school. But when they went off to college and the pros, he went through extraordinary efforts. Archie writes about a time he went to sixty basketball games in a month.

I don't remember my dad coming to many of my games. He certainly did when he was my baseball coach, but I just can't remember him being at any football games. Maybe he was, but it didn't sink in. It also may have been due to his work, or his illness, or the fact that there were five other kids in the family.

I remember always being at Keith's early soccer games. But as he got older, I recall making him bike to the game, and then I would drive a bit later and watch. This really instilled an independent nature in Keith. Keith's team got into some sort of state playoffs one year and the game was about sixty miles away in Canby, Oregon. Keith's teammates assumed he would bicycle to the game. Having Keith bike so much taught him that he could get around without a car, and he commutes by bike in New York City—ten miles each way—to this very day. Plus, he's thirty and has never owned a car. But I also missed some things by not being at his games from the very beginning. Keith was a little slow to develop his athletic skills as a kid. I often didn't feel bad if I was late to many of his games because he didn't play much. But I got to one basketball game at halftime and he was the high scorer for his team. The coach said he was a wild man! Dang, and I missed it!

There was a baseball game I didn't miss, though. After several years of just so-so baseball, we were at William's Field in Corvallis, and Keith just nailed a ball. This thing went into the gap in right center field. What did Keith do? He just stood there for what seemed the longest time admiring it! We still joke about my response—*"RUN!"* He got a stand-up double. Keith and I couldn't have shared that memory if I hadn't gone to that game.

Whether your kid ends up in the pros or just plays youth sports, it is an opportunity to have a lasting connection with your child—just don't ruin this opportunity by making performance more important than having fun.

–13–
Eight Damaging Things Dads Do or Say to their Kids

THE PURPOSE OF many of the trainings I conduct is for teens to take a look at the beliefs they have about themselves. So, where do these beliefs come from? Simple: from events they have experienced. Some of the events these teens experience are huge, life-changing, and, frankly, ordeals I wouldn't wish on anyone. I have heard things about rape, molestation, abuse, and abandonment. But the event could just as well be as small as being teased by other kids or by a teacher. The size of the event is not what's important; it's the size of the beliefs that we make up about ourselves.

What I have heard over and over are stories of how dads have said or done horrible things to their kids. Sometimes these remarks are said innocently enough, but often, these comments are said maliciously and in anger.

Dads, think before you open your mouth! There are consequences to anything you say.

1. "Why can't you be more like your brother/your sister/ the neighbor kids?"
Kids will look for anything to compare themselves to their siblings. You don't need to say this. There can be real damage

done when your child has done something "wrong" and you lash out in anger. Remember, once you say something, you can't take it back. Nothing good comes from this kind of comment.

Besides, every kid is so different and unique. My two sons were so different growing up. These two guys had different personalities from a very early age. Keith was serious, compliant, and focused as a little kid. When Keith was in the first grade, I got after him for not doing his homework one evening. The next morning, he got up an hour early to finish his homework. Boy, I sure felt guilty. Jesse, however, was curious, energetic, and got his way with his smile. These were two different kids, and I needed to treat them differently. What worked for Keith didn't work for Jesse.

Jesse's reaction to being compared to Keith is typical of what I have seen over and over. In high school, Keith got straight A's. Jesse somehow got it in his head that he couldn't compete with straight A's, so he just didn't try at all. By the time Jesse got to the tenth grade, he gave up and began failing.

In Chapter Five, Rick Brand experienced the same comparison issue with his son, Robert. Both Robert and Jesse made up these comparisons on their own. Rick and I didn't overtly make these comparisons, but our sons picked up on subtle hints.

I have seen this giving up in kids all too often. They rationalize that if they can't be as smart, or as athletic, or as talented as their brothers, sisters, or friends, they go the completely opposite way.

2. "Don't be such a sissy. Big boys don't cry."

How many other ways can this be said? I actually heard of one dad who modified his son's name so that it sounded effeminate and then mocked the son at every opportunity. Talk about cruel.

I really thought we were done with this one. Growing up in the '50s and early '60s, I heard this one a lot, especially in sports. The expression was "Suck it up!" Teaching a little toughness is fine, but the idea that boys aren't supposed to cry is ridiculous.

I saw two sports-related examples of this in a matter of days. As I walked by a student's folder at one of the program schools, I saw a picture of Michael Jordan clutching an NBA championship trophy, his head leaning on the trophy. And Michael was crying—yes, crying. The caption read, "Even Big Boys Cry." I thought, Yes! It's changing. This was an old photo, the 1991 championship. Then, not two days later, an article I read about Ken Griffey Jr. shows that the big-boys-don't-cry myth is still alive.

In 1999, Junior asked to be traded from the Seattle Mariners to the Cincinnati Reds. One of the reasons he wanted to be traded was so that he could be closer to his dad, a coach for the Reds at the time, and his own kids.

It broke my heart that he left Seattle, but I understood wanting family time. After eight years of struggling with injuries, the Reds made a rare trip to Seattle in June of 2007 for a three-game series. The Mariners created a Ken Griffey Jr. appreciation day at the first game of the series. The fans just went wild. The fans gave Junior a standing ovation before the game, and again when he came to bat for the first time. In the third game, Junior hit two home runs, and again the fans gave him, a player on the opposing team, a standing ovation each time. But look what he said after the first game. The following was taken from the ESPN Web site:

Keeping his emotions in check was Griffey's toughest

task. *"I looked around, and it was touching. But I didn't want to start crying, so I have to go home and have my kids look at me and say, 'Daddy, you was a punk,'"* Griffey said, grinning toward his three children. *That didn't mean the ceremony and reception didn't become emotional for some of his teammates.*

"To be honest with you, I teared up a few times," said Josh Hamilton, who hit a solo homer in the fifth. "Just the excitement and the welcoming of the crowd. It was something you rarely see. It was just one of those things you are happy you are here to witness it" (Griffey's emotional return to Seattle ends with blowout win).

I thought, Ah, crap. I couldn't believe Junior's comment about what his kids might say. He could have made great inroads to boys being able to show some emotion. Junior, it's okay for grown men to show a little emotion. In fact, I would have thought more of you, not less, if you had let it go, just a little.

The danger of telling a boy not to cry is that the real message is, "Don't ever show *any* emotion. It's a sign of weakness; you're not a man if you show any emotion." Yet I say this over and over in seminars to young men: there is nothing stronger or more powerful than a man with a heart.

I wish more dads would give their sons the same message that First Sergeant Charles Monroe King wrote to his unborn son. This is Sergeant King's first journal entry that appeared in *A Journal for Jordon*.

Be humble about your accomplishments, work harder than the guy next to you; it is alright for boys to cry. Sometimes crying can release a lot of pain and stress. Never be ashamed to cry. It has nothing to do with your manhood (Canedy 6).

3. "You'll never amount to anything."

I have heard this message in many forms: "You are going to end up a crack addict," "You are just a slut," and many other equally cruel remarks. I have seen the damage this kind of comment has on young people. It's unfortunate, but so many teens take these cruel messages to heart and actually start to believe them.

One of the worst such statements was uttered by a dad on his deathbed to his adult daughter. She comes to the hospital to visit her dying dad. She had recently lost a great deal of weight. And what does dad say to her? "You'll never keep it off." When I spoke to this woman years after her dad's death, she said that when she struggled with her weight, she could still hear her dad's negative comment.

Occasionally, very occasionally, this kind of comment will actually inspire kids, but the inspiration does not motivate them to do something for themselves—it is done to spite Dad. Not the way you want really want to inspire. But, more often than not, the kid takes it in as gospel and not only believes it, but starts to behave as if it were true.

4. "I wish you had been a boy."

Dads, you have been given a gift to have a daughter—an adoring little girl who just wants to be daddy's little girl—and then you say something like this! You don't even have to say it though. If you really think and believe this way, it will come out and show in your actions. Remember what I said about your way of *Being*? If you silently wish your daughter were a son, it will show in your behavior. She will get the message one way or another. You think you can hide it, but you cannot—it will ooze out of you.

5. "You are such a slut/fag" or other such cruel name-calling.

Yes, I have actually heard this. The names can be as crude and demeaning as they are endless. Again, the words are usually spoken out of anger or frustration. Think about this: you are calling your own flesh and blood these names. This is your child. No one else's.

6. "We never intended to have you" or "You were a defective condom baby."

Believe it or not, I have actually heard this condom comment from a teen more than once! And you thought some of the other things were bad. How would you have liked your dad to say this to you? Or how about this: "You're not my kid. Your mom had an affair, and I don't know who your dad is." Wow!

I am a proponent of an adage attributed to Eleanor Roosevelt: "No one can make you feel inferior without your consent." But hearing this kind of crude comment from your own dad as a child has got to be devastating.

7. "I don't want you anymore."

This one can be delivered directly and verbally or indirectly through actions. The most common example, at least in the case of actions, is one in which Dad has little, if any, interaction with his kids after he gets remarried and starts a new family. Just imagine: a man has a child or children. He gets divorced, which is hard enough on kids as it is. Then he gets remarried, has more kids, and actually starts being a father to the new kids.

What are his older kids expected to think except there

must be something wrong with me if he is being a dad to other kids.

8. Verbal, emotional, physical, or sexual abuse of their kids, and/or abuse of their wives in front of the kids.

Now, it seems pretty obvious not to abuse or molest your kids, but I have heard kids talk about how their dads beat their moms, threw their moms around the house like rag dolls, or did the same thing to one of their siblings. I have heard kids tell stories of trying to hide—under a table, or behind doors, or in closets—until the rage is over. Other kids tell of how, at ages as young as four, they have tried to intervene—only to become the target of Dad's rage.

Five things your children want to hear from you
1. "Yes"

Use this one when asked things like, "Dad, can we play catch?"; "Dad, can we go to the pool?"; "Hey Dad, look at this!" Your child is asking to spend some time with you: just say yes. Put down your cell phone, step away from your computer, put your work down, and do something with your flesh and blood.

I did an awful lot of things with my son Keith, but occasionally, he likes to remind me of the time he asked me to play catch with him and I said no. His exact quote was: "Can you imagine a dad who wouldn't play catch with his son?"

Remember that earlier, I said my pattern was to promise, "Sure, we'll do it tomorrow," and then not follow through. It was my way of saying, No, I'm not going to do that with you. I'm sure my boys figured out pretty quickly that tomorrow wouldn't come.

Remember the lesson from Chapter Five, when Bill Ogle learned about his dad's disappearance? Bill gets up off of the couch every time his son says, "Hey Dad, look at this!"

2. "I'm proud of you"

Dads, if you are like me, you tend to find fault or to see how your child could have done better, whether it be in sports or in school. How about putting a lid on trying to fix your child and giving him or her a compliment? Look for something your child did well, and acknowledge it. Frankly, this is THE one thing that teens say they want to get more often from their dads.

3. "Good job"

This is like the "I am proud of you," but for small, simple things. Many dads are critical of the jobs done by young children and are quick to find fault rather than see the effort their kids made.

4. "No"

Your job as a dad, and as a parent, is to set boundaries. Too many dads are actually afraid to say this simple, two-letter word to their kids. As fathers, one of our jobs is to prepare our kids for the world. No one else on the planet treats our kids like we do. By this, I mean the reason our kids are so entitled is that we dads give material things and privileges to them without the kids actually earning it. Do your teen a big favor: teach them this simple two-letter word.

5. "I love you"

Why dads don't seem to say this more is a mystery. Maybe it's because we didn't hear it from our dads, or because we think it's a sign of weakness. Whatever it is, let's get over ourselves and teach our kids that dads can express love . . . *through words!*

In the book *Manning*, Archie Manning talks about the lessons he learned from his dad, Buddy. Buddy committed suicide when Archie was a sophomore at Mississippi State. Archie relates that his dad rarely, if ever, said "I love you" to Archie. So Archie says that whenever he says goodbye to any of his three sons—Peyton, Cooper, or Eli—he always tells them he loves them.

–14–

Forgiveness

W HEN I FIRST started working with troubled teens in seminars, I was surprised how many kids were willing to forgive their dads. The teens were willing to forgive the most egregious behavior—dads abusing their wives, dads doing drugs, dads getting arrested, even dads battering or molesting these kids' siblings. Many kids were even willing to forgive dads who had molested *them*. After a while, I just came to expect the teens to be forgiving.

But why? Why would a child be so willing to forgive a person for showing no love and affection towards them? Because the person we are talking about is no ordinary person. This is the one person that a child is able to call "my dad." I don't pretend to be an expert in child psychology or human behavior. I am able to observe, though. Kids want that connection with their biological dads. I've come to believe that having a connection with one's biological parents is a basic human need. I've seen so many adopted kids distance themselves from their adoptive parents. These adopted kids think that there must be something wrong with them if their birth parents gave them up. They also have the thought that if their "real" parents gave them up, these adoptive parents surely will do the same. Some of these kids think if their biological parents didn't love them enough to keep them, then how could anyone love them? Look at how many adopted kids go out searching for their birth parents after they become adults.

I have also seen kids hold back love and affection from their stepparents. I have heard this same excuse from a number of kids: "If I show love to my stepdad, I am being disloyal to my biological dad."

In the following stories, you will read about three people who didn't have an ideal dad. I chose to ask each of these people to share their stories, because I expected all of them to tell the story of their horrible dads and how they affected them. I was surprised to receive stories of forgiveness.

Ray Colello

I heard a fantastic story about Ray, his brother Shane, and his sister Mary before I ever met any of the Colellos. Supposedly, the three siblings were raised by relatives because their dad couldn't afford to raise his kids. When their dad hit a big lottery, the relatives told him to take his three kids. Dad took the kids from his relatives and immediately took them to a program for troubled and out-of-control teens in North Georgia. The story went on to say that Dad hit a big lottery not once, but twice.

When I first met Ray and Shane, I assumed they didn't really deserve to be in a program. Well, that's what I get for making assumptions. The story I heard wasn't totally true—but close.

Ray Colello was born in Trenton, New Jersey, on September 1, 1989, one minute before his twin brother Shane and four months premature. On January 22, 1990, their sister Mary was born.

We lived with our Mom, Betty Colello, our Uncle Woody, and our stepbrother, Tommy. My dad, Raymond Ryel, and my mom never married. Shane and I don't remember much about living with her. But from what we were told, we were abused by our mother. We were also told that we suffered brain damage from the abuse and beatings. My dad's brother, Uncle Vinnie, and his wife, Aunt Suzee, used to pick up the three of us for weekend visits. Uncle Vinny, a police officer in Trenton, first noticed the bruises on the back of Shane's arms and legs. After repeated questions from Uncle Vinny, Shane finally said that Mom did it.

Being a cop, Uncle Vinny initiated an investigation. The investigation revealed that, indeed, Mom was beating us. We were taken from her and lived with Uncle Vinny and Aunt Suzee, who gained partial custody. On Christmas of that year, we were four or maybe five. That's when I met my dad for the first time. Dad wanted custody of the three of us. He had to get blood tests to prove he was our dad. Mom didn't show up for a court hearing, so Dad automatically got full custody of us.

We (me, Shane, Mary, Uncle Vinny, Aunt Suzee, and my dad) spent three years living together in New Jersey. Then we moved to Florida, where we all lived together. Shane and I shared a room, and Mary had one to herself.

When we first moved down to Florida, my dad purchased a new motel. My dad and Aunt Suzee worked together on the hotel. During the first year, they did a lot of work on the hotel and got a beatification award. With Dad working on remodeling and managing the hotel, he wasn't home a lot. I do remember all of us occasionally going to the hotel and just hanging out together.

But, for the most part during these years, I considered my uncle more of a dad than my own father. Uncle Vinnie took us to our basketball games and watched us play. He always got us into sports. He made sure we had our uniforms and would go out and buy us what we needed. Maybe it was because he never had any kids.

But as kids moving from New Jersey to Florida, we didn't know a lot of other kids. Maybe that's why we started to get into a little trouble at school—fights and stuff. At home, Shane and I would fight and wrestle, and we'd get into trouble for that too.

The only time Dad cared was when we got into trouble. He never really made any attempt to show affection.

But things started to escalate as we got into our teens. Shane and I each got arrested once for small stuff.

On June 10, 2005, Dad took us to a specialty school in Georgia. I was failing classes at school. Shane had got arrested, and he was dealing drugs. Mary really didn't have any drug use or bad grades, but she did have a bad attitude. I remember Dad having three bags packed for us one day, and I remember him saying we were going on vacation.

Shane and I accepted the fact we were there and that we deserved to be there. But Mary didn't think she had done anything to be sent away, and she was crying. I was sitting in the old conference room at the specialty school and overheard Dad in the next room. All I remember hearing him say was, "How much until they are all eighteen?" [Author's note: I estimate the check would have been in the order of two hundred thousand *dollars.] Dad just dropped us off because he didn't want to raise us anymore. I guess he could afford to just pay for the school all at once because of the lottery hit before he gained custody of us. [Ray stated that his dad won a $14.5 million lottery some time before he gained custody of his three kids. I confirmed that Ray's dad won $70,786 in a Florida lottery game in August of 2007.]*

For the first couple of months at the school in Georgia, I was bitter. I kept hoping for that first letter from him. Everyone kept telling me that my dad would write, but after awhile, I knew he wouldn't. But there was that hope in the back of my head that the letter would finally come. I held onto this hope for some time. But finally, I just realized there would be no letters.

My first family rep, Rosemary, tried to get my dad to be involved in the program, but Dad apparently wasn't interested. I was there for twenty-six months, and I didn't receive a single letter from my dad or anyone else in my family. I did receive letters from other parents, and it made me happy to know that someone cared. I did have a few very short phone calls with my dad, but we never discussed anything beyond, "Hello, hey, how you doing?" He never attended any of the adult seminars that were offered. He didn't attend the PC (parent-child) seminars. [Seminars are designed to bring the issues to the surface and work on getting them resolved before the teen comes home.]

While Mary was in the program, she was adopted by a member of the school's administrative staff. I had mixed feelings about her adoption. I mean, it was great to see her with a caring family, but I felt like she was being taken away. I was told that if I was doing drugs or involved in illegal activities, I was not welcome at her adoptive dad's house, but I know that in my heart and mind she would always be a Colello. I just couldn't get the thought out of my head: "How can anyone tell me I can't see my own sister?"

Mary graduated the program on August 4, 2007. She is currently living in North Georgia and works at the specialty school the three of us attended.

Shane got kicked out of the school in Georgia and was sent to a boot camp in Mississippi. Then he joined the Army.

I left the program ten days before I turned eighteen to join the Job Corps. I took a few days off from the Job Corps in November 2007 to attend Shane's boot camp graduation in Kentucky. There, I came down with severe abdominal pains, which the doctors thought was appendicitis. Turned out it was a fairly serious intestinal infection. This kept me in the hospital for a few days and knocked me out of the Job Corps.

I then moved in with a program family near Atlanta, where I finished high school through online classes. During this time, I called home and spoke to Dad a few times. We would talk for maybe ten minutes. It was just, "Hey, how you doing? How's the family?" The day I finally finished high school, I called everyone letting them know. The last call I made was to my Aunt Suzee. My dad was there visiting and he said, "That's great." But then he essentially told me never to call there again. It just ruined my day; I was all happy about finishing high school and had called my brother and sister. He was the last person I called. There were no congratulations; it was just, "Don't call here again." I don't know if there was anything behind it or what. But there I was, in a great mood. I had just finished high school with a high GPA. It was just like he didn't care about his own kid. But I learned again that I have to move on without my dad in my life.

I didn't hate him for what he did. Sure, I had anger towards him. But he's old for being a dad. He turned seventy-two in November of 2008. He grew up during the Great Depression, when a father and son didn't really show affection, in a stern and strict home. He didn't grow up in a weak family. I met my grandma, and she was a great person. But I saw how he grew up as a strict person.

I understand where he's coming from. His dad died of cancer before I was born. I can understand how my dad got to be who he was. But I was grateful that I even had a father. He wasn't the greatest, but I did learn from him. I learned to respect people no matter what they were or what they looked like. I also learned to be proud of who I was and what I had. I learned to respect women at a very early age. I was always respectful. I learned to interact with society.

I asked Ray about his mom: where was she? What was she doing during all this time?

People have told me that Mom lives up north (Pennsylvania or New Jersey), and that she does drugs, but it's just stories—they don't really know. I've tried to find out where she's at, but I just don't know where to look. I'd sure love to know where my mom is, and to ask her why. But it would be like opening a healed wound, you *know? We were told by Dad what happened—and if we wanted to find her, that was up to us. I just got used to growing up without a mom.*

Currently, I am living with a family near Atlanta. I work with the dad in his business some. I am weighing my options of finding a career or joining the service. Recently, I have been going to a church group called "Life Hurts, God Heals." It's a program designed to help teens that have lost a family member and teens who are struggling. I initially went so I could learn something and get help for what I have been through, but I have found that I have helped others by telling my story. This group has helped me realize one of my dreams is to help other kids. I'd like to show others it doesn't help to dwell on the past. It's about the here and now, learning from your past, and creating a future of your own.

Ray's story shows just how forgiving kids can be of their dads. I really expected Ray to be angry, bitter, and seriously resentful towards his dad. This story goes to the heart of how much kids are attracted to and seem to need their dads.

Yes, Ray was hurt, but not really angry. I didn't understand this phenomenon of forgiveness towards cruel dads, yet I had heard stories like Ray's all the time. I have come to realize that kids have one dad, and they want that dad to be special. As three- and four-year-olds, we adore our fathers. We think our dads are the greatest. When we get older and realize that our dad is not the dad we hoped for—well, we make excuses, like Ray did. For Ray, his story with his dad remains incomplete. There's still a chance Ray and his dad can have a relationship.

Dan Roach

My dad is a son of a severe alcoholic and womanizer, so, needless to say, he taught me mostly how not to do things as they relate to family and women. He was physically abusive to my mother for ten years until she left when I was five. He had a period of relative sobriety throughout his early thirties, although he had a very abusive and negative attitude toward women. When he was in his late thirties, he was retired due to disability and began to drink heavily and abuse painkillers. During this period, communication with my father was nonexistent, except when he sought advice from me, his youngest. This always occurred while he was out of his mind on pills and booze. The rest of the family would not even deal with him in this state, but I was only in eighth grade and eager to please my father. I was willing to accept any kind of attention, however dysfunctional. We spent many nights discussing life and people, and I willingly gave him the benefit of my vast fourteen years of experience with life.

My dad was not necessarily physically abusive to us like in the movies, although a few times he was. It was more that he was so self-destructive and unstable that it made things very difficult for us. I remember one time when he was up all night drinking, and I awoke to a loud BANG! It turns out that he had thrown a cup of white gasoline into the wood-burning stove and had blown the two-hundred-pound stove about three feet across the room and burned off all of his facial hair. It seems kind of funny now, but at the time it wasn't. Things like that were always happening.

Once, when I came home late from my job in high school, the house was completely dark, and my dad was nowhere to be found. I went on a search and eventually found him lying outside the basement door, directly beneath an open second-story window! We are both not sure what actually happened, but he recalls placing a potted plant on the windowsill on the second floor and then waking up to me helping him up from the basement. Someone or something was clearly looking out for him that night. Not all of the stories are bad, though. Once he took a bar of soap and wrote messages on every window and mirror in the house. He even wrote "Hi" on my glasses. I never quite knew what I was going to come home to. Even to this day, when things are going well for a time, I have to fight the urge to expect something bad to happen.

As time wore on, I became more interested in my own life and even more determined not to end up like my father, who by this time had been arrested several times, attempted suicide several times, and rarely spent a day sober. We all had given up on him and gone our separate ways. My dad often mentions that he was so lonely at that point that he would call the time and temperature recording just to hear a voice. Somewhere along the line, my dad hit rock bottom. I am not sure how or when, but during my second year of college, he announced that he was a member of AA. Needless to say, I was thrilled. Things have not been 100 percent sunshine and daisies since then, however. My dad has had to restart his sobriety twice since, but today he remains committed to it. He has also done a great deal to repair the damage he did over the years. He encouraged and participated in several personal growth seminars with his boys, and even apologized to my mother for the years of abuse he put her through. He has put a lot of effort into making amends.

My relationship with my father, I think now, is a very healthy and mature one. I have a great deal of respect for his efforts and forgive him for his behavior during my childhood. There are many things that he has taught me about how to be a man, and about how to act and not to act, especially toward women. My father has also taught me that it is never too late to make amends, and that nothing is more important than family. I believe that he loves and respects each of his sons. All of us communicate with him on a regular basis and speak openly of those early days. Despite all of the trials we have been through as a family, the lesson that I always remember—and the thing that makes all of it okay and makes me feel close to him—is how to repair an old door hinge with a wooden matchstick. It is a simple task I do quite often, and it always makes me smile and feel like a happy kid who admires his dad. I love my dad a lot, and I am proud to be his son.

Dan's story makes the point that you dads are always teaching your kids something, whether or not you are aware of it, whether or not you want to, whether or not you like it. Thankfully, in Dan's case, he was able to take in some useful lessons and learn from his dad's mistakes. The other thing that comes out of Dan's story for me is, again, just how forgiving sons and daughters can be of their fathers.

Kids also want to please their dads. Dan told me that in

the eighth grade, he would drink with his dad just to gain his dad's acceptance. This just illustrates again how strong the attraction is between kids and their fathers.

Rose Valesco

Rose (or Evelyn, as she called herself when I first met her) is an example of the change and transformation that is available from the program seminars. I met her when I was one of the volunteer staff at her third-level seminar. I initially found her to be a bit shy and unsure of herself. She sure didn't think she was very powerful. Now, after over six years of being involved in the program, she is a certified family coach and facilitator. She works with families of faith, assisting them to lead lives modeled after teachings from the Bible.

> *Looking back, I know now that it's not an excuse, but I see that my dad chose to be a product of his parents. His parents were apparently very physically and verbally abusive. The experience I had growing up—it seemed to me I was living in fear every moment, never knowing when something was going to explode. There are so many things I could say about my dad. He was an alcoholic, he abused us kids, he beat our mom, and he was cheating on her.*
>
> *The one event that stands out for me was when I was about five. I was just sitting on the floor in the living room, just playing, and he walked in, without saying anything. With wholehearted strength, he slapped me across the face, and I went flying across the room. After I recovered and stopped crying, I asked, "Daddy, what did I do wrong?" He said, "That was for just thinking about it." From that day on, I never knew what might set him*

off. He was like a time bomb. Until he died, I was living in fear.

I am the youngest of seven children. The way it went was: my parents had six kids in a row then, they waited six years to have me. I thought that meant I was a mistake. The way my dad treated me reinforced that I was a mistake, a burden. I just wanted to hide in a corner. Whenever one of my siblings got to be eighteen, they split out of the house.

For maybe six months (it felt like just two months) before he died, he started to change. There was only me and one brother living at home at the time. He would laugh with us. He would take us to go and get ice cream, which was unheard of. He bought my mom a car. We were like, "I don't know what's gotten into Dad, but we're liking it." I wish we had more of that from Dad growing up.

One of my strongest memories of him involved me and how I wore my tee shirts back then. I would roll the shirt up between my breasts to make a halter top. He hated that. He would get so mad, and we had arguments; he even beat me for wearing my shirts like that. But once, in those last few months, he called me into his bedroom and sounded like he was almost mad. I thought, Uh oh, what did I do now? When I got to his room, he turned around with his shirt tucked like I wore it and said, "How do I look?" It was hysterical, and we started to laugh together. I had never laughed with him that way.

When I was twelve, I was home alone with Dad. He was eating some chicken and got to coughing. He was in the bathroom for a long time. I was keeping a real close eye on him, as I was watching TV when I wasn't supposed to. After a while, I would knock on the door and ask how he was, but he wouldn't answer. Finally, my mom, sister, and my sister's boyfriend came home. They tried for a long time to get Dad to open the door. Finally, my sister's boyfriend broke the door down. As I was rushing into the bathroom, I literally heard a voice that said, "Don't go in there." It's a good thing. Dad had suffered a brain aneurysm and was slumped into the bathtub. They said his eye looked all black. Everyone who saw him was horrified.

After he had died, I just let go. I had experimented with drugs a little bit before, but I was deathly afraid of my dad catching me. I started to do drugs all the time. I became very promiscuous. I was involved in gangs, and even witnessed murder. Worst of all, I didn't care about myself. I didn't matter, to the point that I let guys beat me up. I figured I didn't even deserve to live. Finally, it got so bad I actually feared for my life, because of one boyfriend. That was the turning point for me. I left him, but he didn't want to let me go. He stalked me for a year and a half. I got a restraining order and made sure I was never alone. I found that the authorities bent over backwards to help any woman who took a stand for herself. They seemed to be used to the woman who said she had had enough and then was back with the guy in a week. I finally just moved—with no notice, so he couldn't find out where I had gone.

It's been a long process, but I have gotten to where I know I am worthy and life is worth living. The belief that I am worthless still comes up from time to time, but I don't let that belief run my life anymore.

It's funny, but when I think back about my dad, I don't usually think about all the abuse and drinking. I think about how he would sit on his bed and watch TV—baseball or football. I pretended to like these sports, just so I could be near him. He would love to order this fried shrimp dish that was just yummy. Whenever he got it, I would hop up on the bed with him. He would say, "I'm not going to give you any of this."

I would just look up at him and say, "Oh, Daddy, I don't want any, I just want to hug you." I would wait awhile. Then I would ask him if I could have some shrimp. I usually did get some.

I know that he hurt me physically and emotionally; he would beat my mom and my siblings to a bleeding pulp. But through all of it, I still loved him. He was Dad. I would have gladly walked across a bed of nails for him. He was the sun and moon to me. I looked up to him so much. I would have done anything to make him happy if I knew how. In fact, there were moments when I think I did make him happy, although they were short-lived. But there were those sparks. In his own way, he loved me. Those are the pieces that I hold onto, those memories.

Every couple of years, my family gets together for a reunion. In the summer of 2011, we are going to get together in Puerto Rico to honor my dad. It will be thirty years since his death, and we want to celebrate his life. Yes, he wasn't an ideal dad. But because of him, I am strong, driven, resilient, patient, and wise in many ways. Instead of talking about the horrors, we are going to talk about the things we learned from him and the things we are grateful for.

-15-

When The Going Gets Tough

ONE OF MY inspirations for writing this book came from a script I read in my seminars. One of the phrases I use is "There's no book on how to be a dad." Well, I thought, I'll just go ahead and write that book on how to be a dad. But that idea didn't last long. As I said at the start of this book, a how-to book has step-by-step instructions for every possible scenario. But I've seen the situation over and over again: good, committed dads doing all they can for their kids, but things don't turn out well—certainly not like the dads had ever imagined.

I swear: you could follow everything I have written in this book; for that matter, you could buy and follow the recommendations of every single book ever written about being a dad; you could have a team of child physiologists follow you around and give you advice every single day . . . and guess what? No matter what you do or say, your child just might not turn out like you had planned or do what you think is the right thing. Everyone is unique, and each person will react differently given the same circumstances. Besides, we're talking about human behavior here. Human behavior is complicated and, oh-so-often, unpredictable.

Now I'm not suggesting that you just throw up your hands

and do nothing. Sometimes your child will do things that will not be anything like what you had planned or hoped for. *You cannot make your child do anything he or she doesn't want to do.*

But what you can do is set clear, strong, and definable boundaries; you can set up consistent consequences; you can teach values and live these values. I also strongly believe that when you stick to your guns, eventually, your children will remember the lessons you have taught them.

Jesse and me

I thought I was one of those dads who had a child who didn't turn out like he had imagined.

Jesse was the cutest little kid you could imagine. He was so cute I thought we should have taken him to do modeling or acting. His crawl as a toddler was just classic. He was cute, and he knew it. In the first grade, his brother Keith, who was in the fifth grade, protected him from all the fifth grade girls who wanted to hug and cuddle him. Jesse would hug his first grade teacher's legs, and she let him get away with the cute act. He got away with so much in the first grade that I discovered at the start of his second grade year that Jesse couldn't read any word over three letters long. I bought *Hooked on Phonics* and spent a year working on his reading. Too bad I made this year-long exercise a misery for Jesse, but he did learn how to read.

I fell for this cute, lovable Jesse myself. I made Keith ride his bike to sports practices and games, but I drove Jesse to his activities. When Jesse showed the least bit of initiative, I fell all over myself complimenting him.

But Jesse was some kind of talented. In the fourth grade, we were told by the school system that Jesse had qualified for the Gifted and Talented education program. Sherry and I were shocked. I may have said something like, "Did they mix up the results with someone else?" It really hurt when Jesse started to go downhill. He got suspended in middle school for being involved in "drug talk." I fought the school and appealed the decision to the school superintendent. Then things really started to go downhill.

We caught him and a friend with pot ready to celebrate April 20 (4-20 is the teen code for pot smoking). Jesse got caught stealing cigars from a local grocery store then got defiant when the police and the store manager questioned him. He started skipping school and stealing beer and money from us. The worst was when he wrecked the house looking for a Nintendo game system we had taken from him. Sherry was so scared she called 9-1-1. Jesse heard her calling, so he slammed the phone down while screaming at her. That brought five screeching cop cars to our house.

Sherry and I tried everything we knew how to do. We took him to our counselor numerous times. He got tested for attention-deficit/hyperactivity disorder (ADHD), but he was just fine. We tried a child psychologist; Jesse refused to go to the appointment. We had an intervention at his high school. The principle, the French teacher, the wrestling coach, Sherry, and I all showed up. Not Jesse, though! I told the principal that if my older son Keith hadn't gone through the same high school before Jesse, I would have blamed the school.

I really wanted to blame the school, because I didn't want to believe that I had anything to do with Jesse's struggles and downhill slide. Keith was fine. Fine, I'm saying—what an understatement. In high school, he got only A's, graduated valedictorian, and didn't do drugs or drink.

Yet there was Jesse, drinking, smoking pot, getting into trouble with the police, and stealing money from us. I questioned every belief I had about my skills as a dad. I was embarrassed to tell anyone about our family struggles. When Sherry and I made the tough decision to remove him from our house, I was crushed.

What had I done wrong? I kept looking for someone to blame, but there was really no one to blame. So I looked at what I did wrong. I really started to beat myself up . . . but then there was straight-A's Keith. It helped a little when someone told me I didn't have any more to do with Keith's straight A's than I did with Jesse's problems with the police.

For a while, after Jesse went away to a program, I kept it to myself. I still thought that people would judge me. I thought that people would talk behind my back. I thought that they would think I was a bad dad.

What I came to understand is that we cannot make decisions for our children. We cannot force our kids down any particular path; all we can do is create boundaries for them. We can give them our advice and counsel. We can teach them our values. What our children do with all of this is up to them. It's like Corvallis High School for my two sons: the school made a lot of activities available to the students, but it was up to the students to decide which, if any, of these activities they would engage in. Keith took advantage of everything that was available; Jesse didn't.

I learned that all the things I had taught Jesse—and all the things that he learned while he was in the program—were still there inside of him. I learned that perhaps these lessons and tools need time to percolate and stew, but what you teach your teen is never wasted—sometimes there is just a delay factor. I don't go to church anymore, but many of the values I learned from my parents, and from being brought up Catholic, are a part of who I am.

Jesse must have been one of those late bloomers. He eventually got his act together. He graduated from high school while in the program. His GPA was over 3.5, and he gave a commencement speech as the honor graduate.

But after eight months back home, things started to go downhill again. He enrolled at Oregon State University and informed us by voice mail, "It's a whole new world." Apparently that meant he could do anything he wanted and could come and go from our house as he pleased.

During his first term at Oregon State, he got a 2.7 GPA without trying, but there was constant turmoil with Sherry and me. He got busted for pot possession and for taking my car without permission. We finally kicked him out of the house and let him fend for himself.

In his second term at Oregon State, Jesse just stopped going to classes and got a 0.0 GPA. He lived with friends for a while. He got evicted from an apartment, after his so-called friends spent his share of the rent. He started couch surfing and sometimes snuck into our garage to sleep.

Jesse eventually earned his way back into our house. He bounced between fast food jobs before he got a certified nurse's aide certificate. He worked at a nursing home for a year and then got a job at the local hospital, where he is now a unit secretary. He enrolled at a community college where he got 3.8 and 4.0 GPA's. He transferred back to OSU after a year and a half. He graduated with a general science degree in March 2009, got married in April 2009, and then enrolled in a nursing program. He did this all on his own dime—he paid for his education himself! Once he found something that was important to him, he did everything in his power to make it happen. This is the power in having kids work for things, rather than giving it all to them.

While my experiences seemed devastating to me, the stories you are about to read are tragic. In all cases, these dads drew on a number of things—including faith, family, friends, and inner strength—to get through their struggles. I included these stories to illustrate that dads know they matter to their children, and to show how these dads responded to difficult situations and continued on after serious tragedy.

I have read and heard a number of versions of the following expression: "We are not judged by the events that happen to us, but by how we respond to the events in our lives." The following stories show just how dads have responded to the tough events that were thrust upon them.

My brother Pat

My brother Pat and I were born at opposite ends of the '50s (he in September 1959 and I in May 1950). Given our age and birth order differences—second versus sixth (and last)—I really didn't have much interaction with him while I lived at home. I accused Pat of being spoiled by my parents. Maybe not so much spoiled, but he and my sister Kat didn't seem to have the strict parents the older four of us had. My brother Richard and I questioned Pat's toughness in sports on a number of occasions. He would show just how tough he was later in life.

After I went to college, I developed a true older-brother relationship with Pat. I started taking Pat to a number of sporting events: an NCAA lacrosse National Championship, an indoor track meet at the University of Maryland, and a U.S. Open golf championship in New York.

Pat was one of my ushers at my wedding when he was just seventeen. When Sherry and I moved to Oregon in 1980 (Pat was twenty and living at home), Pat came with us. Actually, my other brother Richard and I basically browbeat Pat until he agreed to move to Oregon.

Pat really took to the Oregon lifestyle. He nearly immediately started volunteering at a food co-op. He ended up being the produce manager for a long time. He met Jeanne Lund the first summer we lived in Oregon, and they got married the next summer. On August 9, 1981, two days after my fifth wedding anniversary, Pat and Jeanne got married. Their ceremony was unusual, to say the least. It was at the summit of Mary's Peak, a four-thousand-foot mountain about forty miles east of Corvallis. The valley temperature high that day was 109 degrees Fahrenheit.

Pat and Jeanne started a family pretty quickly—Nicole was born in 1982. Pat and Jeanne ended up having five kids: Nicole, Valerie, Daniel, Sarah, and Robert. Two things struck me about Pat during the '80s and '90s. First, that he and Jeanne were able to make ends meet; they kept having kids, and they didn't make a lot of money. For some reason, people seemed to give Pat stuff—big stuff. The number of cars people gave to Pat was amazing. Over the years, I gave him a freezer, two couches, and my utility trailer. The other thing that got my attention was how religious he and Jeanne were. I am still amazed that Pat and I were brought up in the same house, and yet ended up so different in terms of religion. I think this difference kept our socializing to a minimum for a number of years. We often joked that the only time we saw each other was when our parents came out from Maryland to visit.

Their middle child, Daniel, was born not only with Down syndrome, but also with a heart defect. At six months of age, Daniel had open-heart surgery. When I visited them at Oregon Health & Science University in Portland and saw Daniel's chest scar, my knees just about buckled. It was just hard to see such a little, frail baby with such a serious scar.

After years of low-paying, no-benefits jobs, Pat finally got a "professional" job at Good Samaritan Hospital in Corvallis. Pat never seemed to make a lot of money, and Daniel was born with Down syndrome. On top of all this, Jeanne fought inflammatory breast cancer for three years, and during Jeanne's cancer battle, Sarah underwent treatment for lymphoma. I told Pat he reminded me of the biblical story of Job—difficult things kept happening to him, and he just handled it and kept his faith. Here's Pat's story about his son Daniel.

> *Jeanne, Daniel, and I were driving home from Oregon Health & Science University (OHSU) in Portland after spending the day with doctors and undergoing medical tests for Daniel. We were on Interstate 5, somewhere between Portland and Salem. The road was straight and flat, traffic was light, and the sun was low in the west. Jeanne was asleep next to me, or lost in her own thoughts. Daniel, only days old, was asleep in his car seat. It gave me time to contemplate the whirlwind of the last few days, and per my usual train of thought, I boiled it all down to the basics: Daniel was born with Down syndrome. He needed heart surgery, and soon.*
>
> *The heart surgery scared us the most because it was*

the immediate concern. He had two holes in his heart. But he was stable; otherwise they would have scheduled a surgery much sooner. His heart could be repaired, but he would have Downs all of his life. What would that mean?

Jeanne and I were not upset that Daniel had a developmental disability (DD). We loved him unconditionally. I even had a dream while Jeanne was pregnant that we would have a "special" child. We both also had some previous experience working with DD folks. Now, all of those other DD people were more than a face—they were someone's son or daughter. Now one of those folks would be my son. Our son, the person I named after a Biblical hero, and me.

Now what? The questions came faster than any answers. How are we going to pay for this? We had no medical insurance. How are we going to raise him? How are our two daughters going to handle this? Would he grow up and be an enigma? Would he be known as a "retarded kid"? Would he live long enough to grow up? I began to really question my faith. Was there a God? Did I believe He would help us? Was He helping us now? I decided there were problems infinitely harder than what we faced. My faith stayed intact, although shaken.

How did this happen? That is one question I knew the answer to, or, I should say, I knew there was no answer. The doctors made it clear: there is no known cause for Down syndrome.

I continued to mentally sort it all out. Like a flow chart, I would ask myself a question, and explore all possible options. If an outcome was not satisfactory, I moved *back to a previous decision and explored new options to a different conclusion. Too often, the conclusion was too frightening, and I forced myself to move on to another question, or a new question posed itself before I concluded the current one.*

I was processing and rehashing like this when I became overwhelmed and thought that I could handle it no more. Not just the mental gymnastics, but the uncertainty of life ahead. What if I could not cope with all of this? What would happen then? Like all of the others questions, I began exploring all the possibilities, but in an impersonal, almost distant way.

Question: What if I detach myself emotionally? I would still be present, support the family financially (that is a joke!), but remove myself from the pain.

Outcome: I would lose Jeanne's heart. She would be bitter, and carry the burden entirely on herself.

Conclusion: No good.

Question: I could leave the marriage and family altogether. Disappear? Divorce?

Outcome: Same as above, but with a greater burden on Jeanne.

Conclusion: No good.

Question: I could commit suicide.

Outcome: Even worse than above.

Conclusion: No good.

I suddenly realized I was thinking very selfishly up to this point. It was all about me. I am not proud to say that this was really the progression of my thoughts: escape came first. As I watched the sun hanging steady above the hills and the fields losing their detail in the shadows,

I asked myself the question that changed my life: how would I feel had my father left our family because of me?

Outcome: I would have been devastated!

Conclusion: Then what am I going to do?

It was there and then I committed myself to be the best damn dad I could ever be!

While I have too often fallen short of this lofty goal (just ask my kids), I continue to strive to fill their lives with love. All of my children are a blessing to me and have made my life richer. I hope that I do the same for them.

From that point forward, I also made an effort to change the phrasing of my questions. They progressed from, "If I cannot cope . . . " to "If I do not want this outcome, then what do I do?" then finally to "I want this to happen. Now how do I get there?"

I am not sure if I finally just tapped into the paternal instincts that were lying dormant in me or if I finally understood the responsibility that comes with fatherhood. I have heard the term "paradigm shift." I went through more than a shift; it was a transformation.

The transformation was not easy, though, and many times it did not feel permanent. Often, I had to go back to that place in my mind and renew my commitment. And every time I drive that stretch of I-5, I reassess if I am living for me.

A few years ago, I told a good friend that I was a better father because of Daniel, but I was sorry he had to be born with a disability for the change to happen in me. My friend grabbed me by my shirt collar, looked me straight in the eye, and said, "Daniel is a whole person." He continued to explain, in a less dramatic way, that Daniel did *not sacrifice anything for me. He is exactly the way God intended him to be.*

Maybe Daniel was brought to me so I could finally become the person God wanted me to be.

For some reason, Pat's son Daniel and I really made a connection. I think it was the fact that every time Pat's family came to visit us, Daniel and I would sneak to the back bedroom and watch *Free Willy*. Daniel was thrilled when I ended up giving him the videotape. I'm not so sure his brothers and sisters were as thrilled with my gift. Daniel and I are similar in that we can watch a movie over and over. I can listen to the same song over and over, also.

For years I could not understand most of what Daniel said and used his siblings to translate. Then, at a Christmas one year, Daniel came into his own in communication and standing up for himself. Daniel takes everything slowly. I heard one of Pat's friends say we could all do well to live life at Daniel's pace.

Daniel was going ever so slowly opening up his Christmas present from Sherry and me. I offered to help Daniel out with unwrapping the box. Daniel put his hand out to block me and said very firmly and clearly, "No, Bob!" We still talk about that incident.

Daniel now calls me "Bob Dude!" every time he sees me.

After Jeanne's death on her birthday in 2008, Pat has had struggles and challenges. Jeanne homeschooled all of the kids. When she passed away, Robert was just twelve and Sarah was fifteen. Plus, there was Daniel; he would need special care for the rest of his life.

Two months after Jeanne's death, Pat and I were driving together. He was struggling with what to do with Daniel. He was looking at options for him. He was considering a program funded by the local school system. Pat was feeling very guilty. He said he and Jeanne had been committed to not putting Daniel in a public-school setting. He wanted Daniel to be taken care of by family. I sensed he was feeling guilty, and that he felt he was breaking his word to Jeanne. I realized that things were different, but Pat, in the middle of this emotional time, was having a harder time seeing it this way.

Here's an excerpt of an e-mail Pat sent to us, his family, about his struggles after Jeanne's death, and how Daniel was there for him:

> A week or so after Jeanne died; Daniel and I were with a group of people helping prepare the Little League baseball fields for opening day. Daniel was wearing one of my old raincoats, which happened to be the same color as one of Jeanne's coats. Every time I saw him out of the corner of my eye, I thought it was Jeanne. The surge of hope, and then of sadness and disappointment, began to build up without my knowing it. There were more available hands than work to be done, so we left early. I did not make it to the car before the tears came for several minutes. Daniel, the ever-compassionate person he is, just put his hand on my shoulder and hugged me, never saying a word.

Jim Perry

I met Jim and Gay Perry at one of the program seminars I attended in Seattle. They too had a son in the program facility in Mexico. I was amazed at their commitment to the program—they traveled from Houston to Seattle in order to complete their seminars. Like Sherry and I, they were heartbroken about having to send their son to a program. I kept in contact with the Perrys for a time, but then drifted away.

After a few years of not talking to them, I decided to give the Perrys a call. Like I tended to do when I meet old program friends, I asked how their son, Michael, was. Gay told me he was in prison. I was just silent. What can you say? But what she said next was something that just took my breath away: their son was on death row—death row in Texas, of all places. I couldn't begin to imagine what could be going on for the Perrys.

What really amazed me about both Jim and Gay was their mode and attitude. This had to be a nightmare for them. How could any parent imagine this? Jim and Gay told me they feared what other people would say and think, how they would treat them. The Sunday after they got the news about Michael, they considered not going to their regular church service. When they sought advice and told people they weren't going to church, they received support and empathy. They were told they wouldn't be judged for their son's actions.

So they went to church and continued on with their lives as best they could. They continue to be involved with Michael and his appeals. Gay continues to teach preschoolers at their church. Jim has retired and is pursuing a graduate degree in counseling. He also volunteers his time assisting troubled teens that are in juvenile hall or jail.

> This story begins in the 1940s, in Iowa, not on February 24, 2003, when Michael Perry was sentenced to be murdered. I was raised on a small Iowa farm in the '40s, '50s, and '60s. My dad and his dad taught me two things: first,

I was to respect other people; and, second, if I worked hard and never gave up, things would be good. I also remember believing that my dad was invincible and that he would always be there for me. As I journeyed through life, what he taught me served me well. I became more confident that with hard work, I could find and provide all the answers. Well, unknown to me, this was a false confidence.

I married Gay after college graduation and went off to the Army eleven days after our wedding. Two years later, we began married life together in Detroit. It was there that we found out that starting our family was not as easy as we believed, but I felt that I could find the answer. All it would take was hard work and not giving up. After numerous doctor visits, different procedures, and surgery, we found out that some personal beliefs and feelings would have to change. After a lot of questions and self-doubt, we decided to adopt. This wasn't easy for a person from my culture. My culture believed that you got married, had children, and lived happily ever after.

Michael was the second of two sons that we adopted. We loved both of them unconditionally; we just didn't realize it yet. Michael was difficult from the very beginning. As I look back now, that should have been a clue. The adoption agency had told us that his family was just an average Texas family. How untrue this turned out to be. Until Michael was twelve, my job required a lot of travel. It was not uncommon for me to call home at night and hear about the latest event in Michael's life. We never knew what Michael was going to do next.

When my job changed and I was transferred to

Louisiana, we had no idea what lay ahead for us as a family. Shortly after the move, Michael was diagnosed with attention deficit disorder, or ADD. We found a church and began attending church as a family. Because Michael was always misbehaving, we stopped requiring him to attend Sunday school. As time went on, we even stopped going to church because it was just easier than being ashamed of his behavior.

Gay and I started looking for help with Michael's behavior. An ADHD support group, Gay working with his teachers, counseling, parish services, private schools, and private programs were some of the approaches we tried. It was after a failed attempt by Michael to complete an Outward Bound program that I realized I could not find the answers even with hard work by myself. I felt a need for God's help, and I started attending church again. My Christian journey began once more.

It was not an easy choice, but Gay and I decided we needed to get Michael help, even if it was outside of our home. As I said before, this was not something easy for someone from our culture. We wanted to help him—we just did not know how. As Michael went off on his journey, Gay and I began working hard on our Christian journey, not knowing what this would mean to us in the future.

From the age of fifteen, Michael no longer lived in our home. But he was on our minds, in our hearts, and in our prayers. During this same time, Gay and I worked hard on our Christian faith. We studied, asked questions, and prayed for God's guidance in our lives. Our Christian family became very important in our lives. We did not realize what the future had in store for us.

Then it happened. We saw Michael on the 10:00 PM news, being arrested. What had he become involved with? We did not know what was going to happen. Would the news media be at our door in the morning? What would the people in our community think of us? What would the people we know think? Do we go out in public or even go to church on Sunday? The next morning, I called our associate pastor and asked to meet with him. It was during this meeting that I started to understand God's love for us individually. I said to my pastor, "I am feeling confused and messed up inside. I do not approve of Michael's behavior. Even if he is found guilty of murder, I still love him."

My pastor said, "Now you have an idea of how God feels." He was helping me to understand unconditional love. For the first time, I realized what it meant for God's love to have no conditions. Even though Michael was found guilty, I still love him.

Well, we went to church that Sunday. We knew it was where we should have been. Everyone was praying for us, and I could feel God's love in those prayers. I now understand what the Bible says. God does not promise us a life without pain, but he does promise to always be there to help us through our pain. Our Christian family was and still is there helping us through our pain.

Michael's appeal is now going on. He has been diagnosed with bipolar disorder, and we found out that Michael's birth family had a history of bipolar. The history of Michael's biological family was asked for by every one of his doctors. I can only wonder if that bit of information would have made a difference.

> *In summary, my dad and his dad taught me about re-*
> *spect. The respect they taught me did not judge people,*
> *but accepted them as they were. I feel that is uncondi-*
> *tional love, and I pray I taught that to my sons.*

Gary Springer

When Sherry and I moved from Maryland to Oregon, we moved directly across the street from Gary and Ann Springer. Their daughter Mandy was about Keith's age, and we became fast friends.

Gary grew up in rural Oregon and graduated from Oregon State University with a liberal arts degree. He and his dad had a logging business—the degree and his work just didn't seem to match.

Getting to know Gary made me realize what a city boy I was, but Gary was kind and helped me with a lot of practical things, especially how to operate a chain saw and a garden tiller. I knew that Gary worked long, hard hours, but I also saw him as a concerned and dedicated dad. Going through some old pictures of Keith's early childhood, I saw a picture of Gary on his hands and knees giving "pony rides" to the kids.

We lived across from the Springers for almost six years, and then Sherry and I moved back to Maryland for three years. When we moved back to Oregon, we found a new place some three or four miles from the Springers, but there was more than distance separating us, and we saw each other only occasionally. Then Gary and Ann got divorced, and our families drifted apart.

When I was driving home from work one day, Sherry called me on my cell phone to tell me that Scott Springer, Gary's only son, had committed suicide. I still remember exactly where I was. I was stunned, but I really can't begin to imagine what Gary and his family went through, or what got them through this tragedy.

Sometime in the middle of the night of December 5 or 6, 2000, my seventeen-year-old son committed suicide. Scott was a high school senior at the time and was living in Philomath with his mother, Anne. Anne and I had been divorced about six years by then, and I was living in Corvallis.

Anne is a nurse and was working at Good Samaritan Hospital in Corvallis that night and didn't get home until after midnight. She didn't check on Scott until the next morning, when she went to his bedroom to get him up for school. She found him lying on the floor with a plastic bag over his head, and it was tied tight around his neck. She told me later that she didn't comprehend what she saw at first and thought she was looking at "a monster" lying on Scott's bedroom floor.

I was pruning trees on a friend's tree farm several miles away that morning when my sister came to get me and tell me the news. She was in shock and had a hard time telling me Scott was dead. I remember dropping the saw and falling to my knees, and then quickly jumping up again and running for my pickup. I shouted at my sister to go tell my friend who was working some distance away. I raced to Anne's house and stood helpless in the chaos as the police completed their investigation and the local funeral home removed my son's body and hauled it away. I remember feeling angry because the police wouldn't let me go downstairs to Scott's room to see him.

Mandy, my oldest daughter, was a single mom with a five-year-old son, Drew, and was living in Corvallis at the time. Mandy was the first person Anne called after she found Scott on the floor, and Mandy and Drew got to Anne's well ahead of me. Mandy was calm and in charge by the time I arrived, consoling both her mom and Drew, who worshipped his Uncle Scott.

The second hardest thing I faced that day was to find and tell Morgen, Mandy's younger sister. Morgen and Scott were very close. It was a very long, hard day, and I hope to never go through anything like that again or watch anyone I know have to live through it. I couldn't have imagined the trauma of the day beforehand, and I have relived it again and again since.

Suicide is a unique crime in that the punishment for the perpetrator is eternal peace and all who love him or her get a lifetime sentence of sorrow.

I won't go back through the details of all the warning signs Anne and I missed as Scott's mental health deteriorated in the months leading up to the final act. I hope we are both done blaming ourselves for that. Suffice it to say that evidence he left behind in sketchbooks, notepads, and in his computer showed a tortured soul, with demons spinning around in his head that were very real to him. He decided at some point that death was the only escape, the only way out.

I have no doubt that Scott was preparing himself physically and mentally for quite some time before December 5, so he wouldn't risk botching the job ahead. He bought his Christmas presents for the rest of us by Thanksgiving that year, knowing he wouldn't be around to hand them out. I am sure that from Scott's perspective, his clean, relatively painless, successful suicide was the single most important triumph of his young life.

So how did I survive the loss of my son, a loss that seems many times worse since it was by suicide and not in a car wreck, like might happen to a "normal" kid? I honestly do not know. How do you continue to live and function semi-normally when you haven't got a heart anymore?

I remember at some point, not long after Scott's death and the memorial service we held for him, Mandy made Morgen and me swear that we would never take Scott's way out. I didn't want to make that promise, but I knew that both girls would be worried sick about me from that point on if I didn't.

I woke up swearing every single morning for several months after Scott's death. I would literally sit up in bed and yell, "God damn it!" or worse. I wasn't cursing him for what he did. I was swearing because I hadn't managed to somehow die in my sleep, which was my goal when I went to bed the night before. That reaction eventually went away, but getting out of bed has been harder every day since December 6, 2000 than it was before that date. And I haven't had a truly happy, carefree day in the past seven and a half years. Joy died that day, along with my son, and I guess it isn't coming back.

Other unanticipated things have also occurred in my life since my own personal nine/eleven. My daughters and I are closer than we have ever been, and we are ready to drop everything and fly to the rescue if any of us is in any kind of trouble. I cry over every damned thing, *it seems like now. If I hear of a loss of life or traumatic event among family or friends (or even strangers, sometimes), I turn into an instant puddle of tears and runny nose. That can be pretty embarrassing (sometimes in the middle of a meeting, for example!). When I am at work, I work like a demon now—in case it is my last day on the job. When I am at play, I ride my motorcycle at twice the speed limit—in case it is my last day of play. My daughters think I am riding like that as if to create a self-fulfilling prophecy. They confuse my need-to-feel-alive wish with a death wish, I think!*

It upsets the natural order of the world, or at least a family's world, when a father outlives his son. That has now happened to me. My own father is eighty-four and as healthy as a horse. So I have to stick around, at least until he is gone. That means I will only ride my motorcycle at twice the speed limit and not at three times the speed limit—which I have done once, and it scared the crap out of me!

I survived and moved on, following Scott's suicide, because I had no other choice, given the obligations I have to family, friends, and colleagues who depend on and care about me. In that sense, everyone I know personally rescued me after December 6, 2000.

But I am still at risk, still vulnerable. There are times when I feel tired of life, through with life. But I'm not, and I made a promise. So I struggle on.

Doug Taylor

I was introduced to Doug by my longtime friend and fellow football referee, Sam. Sam takes me golfing once in a while.

Sam and Doug have played golf together quite a lot. Once, when Sam was on the golf course with Doug, some guy was complaining about his bad day. Doug quietly told Sam, "This guy doesn't know what a bad day is."

Doug's son Mike committed suicide in 1997, at the age of twenty-seven.

My wife Cheryl and I grew up and went to school in Lebanon, Oregon. During the summers, I worked in the lumber mill in Sweet Home. As a teen, I thought I saw the world pass through that mill, as there were some characters working there.

I decided I wanted to see the world, so I went to college in Corvallis, Oregon, twenty miles west across the Willamette Valley. I got a degree in pharmacy, went to work for Fred Meyer in Corvallis, and retired in Corvallis. So much for seeing the world!

I have three laminated pictures of my kids at their best. Tracy, my oldest daughter (born in 1967), is in her golf follow-through. Tracy is very competitive; she was ready to compete in everything. She won the Oregon State high school championship her sophomore year. She was a member of the America's Cup—kind of the Oregon High School Ryder Cup team—that competed against the Northwest state teams.

Mike's picture is of him as an adult, standing on a porch in the winter. He's with a Down syndrome kid. Mike's greatest pleasure was helping people who really needed help. Mike was an excellent athlete, but he was very non-competitive. He played only for fun. The idea of playing to beat someone didn't make sense; playing to win was foreign to him. He could hit a drive three hundred yards, and he could out-hit his older sister. But he just gave up golf. Why Mike and his sister were so different when it came to competitiveness is beyond me.

Jeff (born in 1971) is in midair, grabbing onto his skateboard. Jeff won the West Coast Regional Vertical Championship twice and went to the national tournament once. Jeff was also competitive, not quite as much as his sister, but still pretty competitive.

When Mike was nine, he and I were playing golf and Mike was on pace to have his best round ever. On the eighth hole, he hit a great drive. As we were walking down the fairway, a squirrel ran in front of us and up a tree. He was just this bubbling little kid and went running after the squirrel. He even tried to climb the tree after him. After that, he didn't care about his round of golf. This is how he approached life—he just lived in the moment.

Both Mike and Jeff got involved in skateboarding. Mike was a good skater, but not quite as good as his younger brother. I got involved with the Boy Scouts and we built a sixteen-foot wooden skateboarding ramp in Avery Park. But the skateboarding seemed to get Mike into trouble. In fact, Mike got into a lot of trouble in those days—probably more than my wife and I realized.

We probably weren't strict enough with our kids, but when my wife and I were growing up, we were given a lot of freedom by our parents. We ran loose, we made good decisions, and we never got into trouble. We thought our kids would likewise make good decisions. We were wrong.

The boys got into trouble with the police when they

were in the eighth or ninth grade. Apparently, a small deli near the Oregon State campus was left open after closing. When word got out, kids were running in and out of the deli, helping themselves to beer. Of course the cops showed up. Jeff was a phenomenal skate boarder, so he jumped on his board and got right out of there. But Mike was a little slower. The police recognized Mike for the good things he had done and yelled, "Mike Taylor! I see you! You better come back here!" Mike went back and, of course, told on his brother.

Then things got worse for Mike. We got a phone call from the counselor at school. She wanted us to come out to the school and talk about Mike. Now Mike was very health-conscious. He was working on being a vegetarian, he exercised regularly, and he hiked and just took real good care of himself. On the way out there, my wife made the comment, "Well at least we know it's not about drugs." But it was—it was LSD. Things continued to get worse. We worked on getting him to reduce and stop his drug use. Even now, I don't know how successful we were in reducing his drug use.

He started college here at Oregon State, living in an apartment that we owned. He got more and more irrational. At the start of college he was very irrational, yet he got a 3.9 GPA in his first term. Turned out he was drunk every day that term. That's how smart he could be when he wanted to.

My wife and I spent a lot of time with him that year, getting him to go to psychiatrists. But by this time, he had decided he needed to commit suicide. He was such an environmentalist that he believed the only way not to do damage to the planet was to not be here. I thought, what do I do now? How can I help him?

By this time, he had been in the psychiatric unit at Good Samaritan Hospital two or three times. One day I was at work when I got a call that Mike was announcing to his friends that he was going to commit suicide that day. My wife was out of town, so I knew I had to do something. I called a pharmacist to fill in for me. I came home and Mike was there, announcing what he was going to do. I called the police and when they came, they said he was too rational for them to do anything. So then I called his psychiatrist, and the police talked to the psychiatrist. Once off the phone, one of the police officers said, "Okay, Mike, I'm going to take you up to the psych ward at the hospital."

Mike said, "No you're not." He and I wrestled Mike to the floor, handcuffed him, carried him out to the car, and took him to the hospital. They kept him at the hospital for a few days and then pronounced him well. Mike was an actor, and he knew the score.

What we learned when we were in the Alliance for Mental Health in Benton County was that, first, most mental illnesses start in the teen years, and, second, that people will often self-medicate. That's what he did.

Mike said he could teach the classes since he knew more than the teachers. Mike also said he couldn't handle the crowds at registration. So he quit college. He went to work for the Bonney Activity Center, a group that works with the physically and mentally handicapped. He worked for them for years.

In Corvallis he met the girl of his dreams, Vanessa. She

was from Minnesota, going to school at Oregon State. Mike worked while she went to school. Then she went back to Minnesota to continue school, and Mike went with her. We drove back to Minnesota one summer to visit. They were in an apartment, and he was doing okay. They eventually got married in Minnesota.

Vanessa was a bit of a radical herself. They got arrested—or, at least, got into a lot of trouble—when they went to some military silo in northern North Dakota with a photographer friend.

They eventually moved back to Oregon. When they moved back, Mike rode his bike from Minnesota to Oregon—he had so much energy. He went up into Canada from Minnesota and rode across Canada. He should have written a book. He rode a recumbent bike. He told stories of riding down the Rockies going sixty-five to seventy miles per hour. He said cars would go by and people were just amazed. He said he bummed places to stay to sleep at night with really strange people. He took the ferry to Victoria, BC, rode down the Washington and Oregon coasts. His favorite place was the top of Mary's Peak, so he rode up there before he came back to Corvallis.

Another time, he rode a freight train to California. He said once he was on top of a rail car when it came to a tunnel. Turns out the tunnel was eleven miles long. With all that smoke, he really thought he was going to die. Once he rode his bike over the Cascades to Sun River, Oregon—one hundred miles. The next day we went to South Twin Lake (ninety-nine acres), and he swam across the lake and back. Then the next day he walked up to the top of South Sister (10,363 feet) and back.

He once took Vanessa to South Sister and they watched the sun go down. Then, what do you do at ten thousand feet after the sun goes down? You hike out—and that's what they did.

I have a picture of the first time he and a friend went to the top of South Sister. They rode their bikes and just kept going with their bikes. When they got up to the top, what did they do? They rode their bikes down the glacier and ice.

But when Mike and Vanessa got back to Oregon, things started to unravel. Mike again worked while she went to school. One summer, Vanessa went to South America to study Spanish. Apparently, a guy she went with was her lover. When she came back from South America, Mike started noticing things. So one day while at work, he finished his duties at work and then went to spy on her. He felt bad for spying on her, but his fears were confirmed.

Then Vanessa announced that she was leaving Mike. Mike said she had taken everything that was important to him—herself. So he was going to take way everything that was important to her—her things. So he proceeded to destroy her stuff in their apartment. She called the police, and they told her it's not against the law to destroy your own property.

I got him home, and eventually he moved in with a friend. Vanessa kept trying to deliver the divorce papers to him, unsuccessfully. Mike didn't want the divorce, so he avoided her. So she had her lawyer deliver the papers to me, at my home! I took the papers back and told them it wasn't my job to deliver the papers. Finally she gave in, paid thirty-five dollars, and the divorce papers were delivered to Mike by the police.

He seemed to get his act together. He bought himself a car and fixed it up. Then he drove to California and applied to nursing school. About two or three weeks later, he came home and told me a story about being in an interview. During the interview, he said, he couldn't even hear them; it was like he wasn't even there. So he just walked out and came home. We again worked on getting him under control.

One night he told us he was going to see his roommate. He told his roommate he was coming to see us. That was the night he took a six-pack of beer, ran the exhaust from the car inside, and just wrote. He wrote Cheryl and me, thanking us for all the things we tried to do. As he got drunker and drunker and the carbon monoxide took over, you could see it in his writing.

I was at work when a man approached the counter and asked for me. He said, "Mr. Taylor, I am the minister from Benton County." He was accompanied by my neighbor Brian. Now I'm not too bright, but I knew right away why he was there.

I closed the pharmacy and walked out of the store with my neighbor, in a fog. I thought we were going to his car, and he thought I was going to my car. Under other circumstances, this would have been funny. Finally, we get into my car and make it back to my house. A short time later, my wife comes home; I think she knew already. Then the minster wants to know where Mike's wife is, and frankly, I don't know. He gets on the phone in the other room and starts making calls trying to find

Vanessa. Finally, I tell the minister I don't want her here now. I thank him for his efforts and ask him to do it somewhere else.

I did meet with Vanessa and told her I didn't blame her for anything. Her family from Minnesota came and hung out for a while. One night they were all over at our house, and I said that Mike's car was hers now. She acted surprised and said, "It is?" Within five minutes, the entire family was gone to check out the car.

But it gets worse. I don't remember if it was that night or the next night. We got to bed and at 2:30 AM, the phone rings, and it's the police. They wanted to speak to Mike Taylor. I didn't know what to say, I don't remember what I said exactly, He's deceased, dead, or what. I asked what this was all about. He said we just picked up so-and-so driving Mike's car, and he was drunk. "We didn't know if he stole the car or if he had Mike's permission to drive it." Turns out, the individual driving Mike's car was Vanessa's new lover.

I remember her stepdad made a comment that Vanessa was Mike's widow. I made the decision that she was actually Mike's ex-wife. I don't need her to be my son's widow anymore. As far as I was concerned, she was the ex-wife that dumped him and pushed him over the edge. But he was teetering on the edge for ten or fifteen years before he met her. I could make the point that we got ten years—wonderful years—of Mike's life because of her. I can go there, and I cannot blame her for Mike's final demise. But she played a part in it, and now she's gone. I don't need her to be part of my life anymore. If they had had children, it would have been a different story. I don't *know where she is now or what she is doing, and I don't care. I don't spend a lot of energy thinking about her. I spend my energy thinking of all the good things about Mike.*

It's not like we weren't prepared for his suicide. He had attempted it on a number of occasions. After he got out of the psych ward, I asked a counselor what we could do to prevent his suicide. He said we shouldn't worry about him committing suicide. I asked why, and he said, "Because he has no history; people that commit suicide have a history." I said, "Well, what about the time he tried it with his car and he didn't know how to hook up the hoses?" He said, "Oh, that doesn't count when they are in high school." I asked about the time he took an overdose of drugs, when he got up in the middle of the night and told someone he was going into the woods to die, when we called the police and we all went looking for him and finally found him. That time didn't count because he was in high school. The time with the car didn't count because he had no witnesses. The third time— I don't remember why it didn't count, according to this guy. I don't know if I let my guard down, or if I was worn down fighting it for twelve years.

How did I get through it? I talked to people. My wife and I never blamed each other, criticized or found fault in each other. In our time with the Alliance for the Mentally Ill, I can think of only two other couples that didn't get divorced. It seems it's just too much stress to handle. One of the things I am most proud of is that my wife and I are still married.

When I retired from a city committee, they said they

were really going to miss my calm logic. I guess I have never been an emotional person.

I really don't know how I got through it. I just took one step at a time and did what I had to do. I probably spent more time worrying about my wife and asking how she was doing.

What made getting past Mike's suicide even tougher was Jeff's reaction. It didn't start right away; I guess it had to fester awhile. He was very open about what poor parents we were. Jeff blamed us, openly blamed us. He thought we should have been stricter. We admitted we could have been, but hindsight is perfect. We felt we made the best decisions we could, given the information we had, and given our personalities. Okay, we were wrong; we're sorry we were wrong, but there's nothing we can do about it.

This felt almost as bad as Mike's suicide. I felt like I was losing another son.

Fortunately, our daughter is very attentive. She takes care of us emotionally, financially, and physically. I just took Jeff's criticism and tried to explain things to him. Basically, we just stopped talking about Mike. We swept it under the rug, I guess you could say.

When Jeff and his wife had a little boy, they wouldn't let anyone babysit except for my wife. One day they called my wife to babysit, but she couldn't go, so she sent me. Jeff was livid: how could I expect to take care of a three-month-old when I hadn't spent any time with him? I did have three kids of my own. Now they bring all three of their kids over here and drop them off, even if I'm the only one here. He now understands the pressure of bringing up three kids and keeping up with them.

Grandkids are just awfully special. You know, we screwed it up the first time—maybe. You can't screw up being a grandparent. Our job is to just love these little kids. It's the parents' job to raise the kids and teach them. I love the role of being a grandparent. I like to have a golfing buddy, and I like to compare which of us is the better grandparent.

About six months after Mike's death, I was in a golf tournament in Portland where I met Mike W., who worked with my son-in-law. He came to me and said he had heard about our son. He said he wanted to tell me about his sons. He had twins that lived only two days. Later, I found out he never talks about those twins, never tells anybody about them. I made a comment. "Oh my gosh," I said, "at least we had a lot of time with Mike; sure, he was a pain in the butt a lot. Those twins were never a pain in the butt, were they?"

He said, "No, they weren't," and that kind of ended the conversation.

Something I have to say is, my wife was amazed at this. The five years after Mike's death was perhaps the best golf I ever played. I played competitively, and when you play competitively, golf is very important, isn't it? Well, golf wasn't so important anymore for me. I would just say, I'm just going to hit this, and I hit it well. It's like I got into a vacuum, because I either had to not think about Mike and not think about anything and go on automatic, or I had to go home. I knew if I went home, I would be miserable. So probably that was one way I got through it. I guess I went on automatic pilot.

So now I'm back to thinking too much, trying too hard to play golf.

–16–

My Dad and Me

ARLIER, I SAID I decided to write this book because of all the dad issues I witnessed in my seminars. When kids were open and showed the hurt of not having their dads, I could literally feel their pain. I felt their ache, their sadness, their loneliness. I often wondered why I felt such empathy when my dad was always in my life; he still is. But I often find myself short, irritated, and embarrassed around my dad. My son Jesse has pointed my behavior out to me. Boy, what am I teaching him about how to treat his dad?

My dad is eighty-seven. He is nearly blind, and he doesn't hear very well either. He forgets things that I told him minutes before and is starting to really show his age.

Yet, without him, I wouldn't be who I am! I wouldn't even be here. I am like him in so many ways. I make silly remarks in public; I say some of the same things he does. I talk a lot and repeat myself, just like him. Sometimes I catch myself when I make a noise or utter something just like him. I even sneeze like him.

As I wrote this book, I realized I had gone through the same stages that I witness in the teens in my seminars. When I was a little kid, I thought my dad was great. I relished the alone time we had. There were things that started to change how I felt about my dad. There were a number of little incidents: Dad not being in my hospital room after surgery when I was four, Dad squirting me with a hose when I was five, not getting Dad's attention because of my siblings, Dad's work, Dad's illness. Once, I got detained for shoplifting candy from the Air Force Base Post Exchange (PX). When Dad picked me up, he told me how embarrassed he was. Rather than going home, he took me straight to the Catholic Church where I took confession. I really felt like I had let him down. As I look back now, these seem to be insignificant events. But, as a young child, I started to think that Dad didn't care and that I wasn't special.

As a teen, I battled with everyone at home, even Dad. He seemed to be the one person who had some control over me. Once, though, I got sent to my aunt and uncle's for a week because I was so out of control at home. As I became a young adult, Dad and I argued about politics—he backed Nixon and the Vietnam War; I didn't.

Yet as I write this book and look back at what he did for me and how I depended upon him, I am amazed. Dad took me to my first Major League baseball and NFL games. When I tried out for high school football as a junior, he said he would pay for my cleats if I made first string on the junior varsity team. I made the varsity team, starting tight end, number 84.

He helped me buy a bike and my first car. When I unsuccessfully applied to the U.S. Naval Academy, he offered to get me accepted to the U.S. Air Force Academy in Colorado. My pride and stubbornness wouldn't even let me consider the Air Force Academy option. When I was in college, I received a monthly check from the U.S. government because Dad was a disabled veteran. I once joked out loud about getting my disability check. Dad got mad, and I think he was hurt by my comment.

My dad taught me about working hard to provide for a family. He was in the Air Force until I was about ten. He retired after twenty years in the Army Air Corp and the Air Force. He then worked in a series of different occupations. He was a salesman, and then a manager at Kinney Shoes. Every time I buy shoes, I think how much better the service my dad provided to his customers was. He went to Benjamin Franklin University in Washington, DC and studied accounting. He then worked at the Government Printing Office. During my high school years, he stopped working because of a variety of ailments, most notably Ménière's Syndrome. This is an inner ear problem that caused his serious, random dizziness. I can recall him lying in bed, just miserable because everything kept spinning.

When Sherry and I decided to get married, he arranged for our wedding and reception to be held at my old Catholic church. When I was trying to build a removable bed for my Econoline van, he was the first person I called when it didn't turn out right.

Who I am is a result of all my past experiences and relationships. I wouldn't be who I am without having gone through every event in my life. That's why we humans are uniquely different. No one—I mean no one at all—has had the same experiences and life I have had. A big part of my life experiences, a very big part, is my dad. I am practical, hardworking (most of the time), funny (at least I think so), and I like structure.

I do love my dad, and I am finally starting to appreciate how much he has influenced and cared for me. I send my dad cards on his birthday and call him on Father's Day. Sherry and I always send him Christmas presents. When I am on a business trip to Florida, I drop in to visit for a day or two. Yet I know I am holding back emotionally.

It's taken me some time, but I do get that my dad matters very much to me. My hope is that this book will also help you realize how your dad matters to you. And for you dads, just how much you matter as a dad.

Acknowledgments

I WISH TO thank my immediate family for all they have done over the years to assist me in completing this book. For over thirty years, my wife, Sherry, has allowed me to do a lot of things to find myself. These things included quitting my engineering job to go to airplane mechanics school (that lasted two months), moving across the country several times, taking numerous trainings, quitting my secure engineering job (again) to become a seminar facilitator, and moving to Utah for a year by myself. She also *convinced* me to become a dad.

My sons Keith and Jesse allowed me to experience the highs and lows of fatherhood. The highs most certainly make the lows bearable.

Finally, I want to thank the teens and the parents of the program. Your willingness to open up and share your hurt and pain allowed me to see and feel how important dads are. Seeing and hearing your stories was the final push I needed to write this book.

There are so many more people I would like to acknowledge. If I included the list here, I'm sure I would forget someone. I have included a full list of acknowledgments on my Web site: www.bobhazleton.com. There, I can add to and update my acknowledgments.

Bibliography

"3rd Man Dies In Shooting At Largo Retail Center." February 5, 2008. Avis Thomas-Lester and Ruben Castaneda. The Washington Post. <http://www.washingtonpost.com/wp-dyn/content/article/2008/02/04/AR2008020400962.html?nav=rss_metro>.

Albom, Mitch. *Tuesdays with Morrie*. New York: Broadway Books, 1997.

Committee on Injury, Violence, and Poison Prevention and Committee on Adolescence. AAP Policy. American Academy of Pediatrics. 6 December 2006. 8 April 2009 <http://aappolicy.aappublications.org/cgi/content/full/pediatrics;118/6/2570>.

Blackstone, Richard. "Fossett Search Reopens Old Mystery." 7 October 2007. *CBS News*. 8 January 2008 <http://www.cbsnews.com/stories/2007/10/07/eveningnews/main3340195.shtml>.

Burroughs, Augusten. *A Wolf at the Table*. New York: St. Martin's Press, 2008.

Candy, Dana. *A Journal for Jordon*. New York: Crown Publishers, 2008.

Canfield, Jack and Mark Victor Hansen. *Chicken Soup for the Soul, The Wisdom of Dads*. Cos Cob, CT: Chicken Soup for the Soul Publishing, 2008.

"Cops: Dad Arrested for Taping Packers Jersey to Son, 7." January 18, 2008, *Associated Press*, <http://www.foxnews.com/story/0,2933,323368,00.html>.

Cosby, Bill. "Cosby, Poussaint On Merits Of Two Parents." *NPR*. Renee Montaine. 19 January 2009.

Cosby, Bill and Poussaint, Alvin F. *Come On People*. Nashville, TN: Thomas Nelson, 2007.

Covey, Stephen R. *The 7 Habits of Highly Effective People*. New York: Simon and Schuster, 1990.

Dungy, Tony. *Quiet Strength: The Principles, Practices & Priorities of a Winning Life*. Carol Stream, IL: Tyndale House Publishers, 2007.

Dyer, Dr. Wayne W. *Everyday Wisdom*. Carlsbad, CA: Hay House, Inc., 2003.

Ford, Henry. *Quotations Page.com*. 10 April 2009 <http://www.quotationspage.com/quote/2330.html>.

"Father's Day Card." *American Greetings*. Cleveland: American Greetings, 2008.

Frankl, Victor. *Man's Search for Meaning*. Boston: Beacon Press, 1984.

Friedman, Thomas L. *The World Is Flat*. New York: Picador/ Farrar, Straus and Giroux, 2007.

Gladwell, Malcolm. *Blink*. New York, Little Brown and Company, 2008.

Gonzales, Richard. "Search for Fossett Turns Up Other Planes. " 11 September 2007. *NPR*. 12 September 2007 <http://www.npr.org/templates/story/story.php?storyId=14330134>.

"Griffey's emotional return to Seattle ends with blowout win." 22 June 2007. *ESPN.com*. ESPN MLB. 23 June 2007 <http://sports.espn.go.com/mlb/recap?gameId=270622112>.

Jacobsen, Peter. *Buried Lies*. New York: G.P. Putnam's Sons, 1993.

"Karl Malone falls short, as a father." 12 May 2008. From *ESPN Page 2*. Hill, Jemele. <http://sports.espn.go.com/espn/page2/story?page=hill/080507&lpos=spotlight&lid=tab7pos1>.

Martin, Roland. "Commentary: Black men must reclaim our children." *CNN.com*. 11 December 2007. <http://www.cnn.com/2007/US/12/11/roland.martin/index.html>.

Millan, Cesar. "The Dog Whisperer: What Your Pet Can Teach You." *Parade*. 11 January 2009: 10.

Millan, Cesar. *Be the Pack Leader*. New York: Three Rivers Press, 2007.

"Nevada high school football recruit made up story." February 7, 2008. Associated Press. <http://sports.espn.go.com/ncaa/recruiting/football/news/story?id=3234302>.

Obama, Barack. *Dreams From My Father.* New York, NY: Random House, Inc., 1995.

Opus strip, June 10, 2007: "Davie Dinkle has two dads."

Roosevelt, Eleanor. *This is My Life.* New York: Garden City, 1939.

"Rose and Raspberries." *Roses to dad.* Corvallis: *Corvallis Gazette Times*, 12 June 2008.

Ruiz, Don Miguel. *The Four Agreements.* San Rafael, California: Amber-Allen Publishing, 1997.

Saxbe, Darby. "Between a Talk and a Hard Place." *The Oprah Magazine.* March 2009: 151.

Sheff, David. *beautiful boy.* Boston New York: Mariner Books Houghton Mifflin Harcourt, 2008.

"Soldier surprises his six year old in class." 25 January 2008. From NBC Nightly News. *You Tube.* <http://www.youtube.com/watch?v=UKWEphP2_Nw>.

Sollabec, Michael. *Urban Dictionary.* 26 January 2006. 5 April 2009 <http://www.urbandictionary.com/author.php?author=Michael+Sollabec>.

Additional Reading

In writing *Dads Matter*, I read quite a number of books. Here is a partial list of those books—including some I listed in the bibliography—and a few comments.

Albom, Mitch. *Tuesdays with Morrie*. New York: Broadway Books, 1997. This is a great little book about Morrie Schwartz who died from amyotrophic lateral sclerosis (ALS), Lou Gehrig's disease. Morrie, a life-long teacher, through Mitch Albom, provides simple yet effective life lessons.

Burroughs, Augusten. *A Wolf at the Table*. New York: St. Martin's Press, 2008 and Burroughs, Augusten, *Running with Scissors*, New York, St. Martin's Press, 2002. I really liked Augusten Burroughs's writing. In these two books, he describes life in a seriously dysfunctional family in great detail. In *A Wolf at the Table* he focuses on his relationship with his dad, if you would call it a relationship.

Canedy, Dana. *A Journal for Jordon*. New York: Crown Publishers, 2008. Dana's husband, Sergeant Charles King, started a journal while being deployed in Iraq, just in case. After he died when a bomb exploded beneath his armored vehicle, Dana decided to write this very touching book for their infant son.

Cosby, Bill and Poussaint, Alvin F. *Come On People.* Nashville, TN: Thomas Nelson, 2007. I haven't read this yet but I love the subtitle; From Victims to Victors and some of the chapter titles including; Turn off the TV, Reject Victimhood, and Give Fatherhood a Second Chance.

Covey, Stepehen R. *The 7 Habits of Highly Effective Families.* Macmillan, 1997. I read this some time ago, but Covey's seven habits stand the test of time.

Dungy, Tony. *Quiet Strength: The Principles, Practices & Priorities of a Winning Life.* Carol Stream, IL: Tyndale House Publishers, 2007. This is not only about Tony Dungy's football coaching career, but also about his early influences including his dad. Near the end of the book, Coach Dungy opens up about his son's suicide.

Dyer, Dr. Wayne W. *Everyday Wisdom.* Carlsbad, CA: Hay House, Inc., 2003. A great little pocket book. I simply read two pages, a sentence on each page, as I start my day.

Friedman, Thomas L. *The World Is Flat.* New York: Picador/ Farrar, Straus and Giroux, 2007. A big book that covers a lot of topics. He makes a big point on how important education of our youth is.

Gladwell, Malcolm. *The Tipping Point.* Boston: Back Bay Books, 2002; Gladwell, Malcolm. *Blink.* New York: Little Brown and Co., 2005; and Gladwell, Malcolm. *Outliers.* New York: Little Brown and Co., 2008. I just love all of Gladwell's books. I think he is a fabulous writer, and I just buzzed through all three of these books. He covers interesting subjects on how society and human minds work.

In *Outliers* he, like Freidman, stresses the importance of education.

Jacobsen, Peter. *Buried Lies.* New York: G.P. Putnam's Sons, 1993. The stories are a bit dated and there seems to be an endless supply of corny clichés, however, Peter Jacobsen does talk about the influence of his dad, the important of families, and the need for dads to let their kids have fun playing golf.

Millan, Cesar. *Be the Pack Leader.* New York: Three Rivers Press, 2007. Cesar claims that this is a dog book. For me, it is a book about taking charge of your life and can easily be applied to being a dad.

Pausch, Randy. *The Last Lecture.* New York: Hyperion, 2008. If there is one book to read in this section this is it. If you don't read his book watch his lecture at http://www.cmu. edu/uls/journeys/randy-pausch/index.html. Here's a professor of computer science dying of pancreatic cancer, and he decides to make one last lecture for his children. If the rest of us could live with a fraction of his energy, with his passion and his dreams, what a different world we would live in.

Sheff, David. *beautiful boy.* Boston New York: Mariner Books Houghton Mifflin Harcourt, 2008. This is David Sheff's view of his son's meth addiction. My son Jesse's drug issues were minor in comparison, but the stories were eerily similar to stories I heard over and over from parents and teens in the program. David's reaction to his son, Nic's downward spiral might as well have been mine.

Printed in the United States
154057LV00003B/3/P